NIMA SANANDAJI

Debunking Utopia

EXPOSING THE MYTH OF NORDIC SOCIALISM

WND Books

Debunking Utopia

Published by WND Books, Washington, D.C. WND Books is a registered trademark of WorldNetDaily.com, Inc. ("WND")

Cover designed by Vi Yen Nguyen

WND Books are available at special discounts for bulk purchases. WND Books also publishes books in electronic formats. For more information call (541) 474-1776, e-mail orders@wndbooks.com, or visit www.wndbooks.com.

Hardcover ISBN: 978-1-944229-39-9
eBook ISBN: 978-1-944229-40-5

Library of Congress Cataloging-in-Publication Data
Names: Sanandaji, Nima, 1981- author.
Title: Debunking utopia : exposing the myth of Nordic socialism / Dr. Nima
    Sanandaji.
Description: Washington, D.C. : WND Books, [2016]
Identifiers: LCCN 2016013123 | ISBN 9781944229399 (pbk.)
Subjects: LCSH: Socialism--Scandinavia. | Welfare state--Scandinavia. |
    Scandinavia--Social policy. | Scandinavia--Economic policy. |
    Scandinavia--Politics and government.
Classification: LCC HX318.5 .S26 2016 | DDC 335.50948--dc23
LC record available at https://lccn.loc.gov/2016013123

Printed in the United States of America
16 17 18 19 20 21 PAH 9 8 7 6 5 4 3 2 1

Contents

Introduction 1

PART 1: THE NORDIC SHANGRI-LA

1   American Obsession with Nordic Social Democracy 17

2   Nordic Success Predates Large Welfare States. 26

PART 2: THE NORDIC CULTURE OF SUCCESS

3   Coffee-Consuming Workaholics 45

4   Comparing Apples to Apples 58

5   How Can the Nordics Tax So Much? 69

PART 3: THE FAILURE OF NORDIC SOCIALISM

6   Nordic Free-Market Success and the Failure of Third-Way Socialism 83

7   Why Are So Few Nordic Women at the Top? 106

PART 4: WELFARE POVERTY

8   The Generous Welfare Trap................................. 125

9   Where Does the American Dream Come True?.................... 146

10   Sweden's Self-Inflicted Immigration Crisis........................ 167

11   Where Are Nordic Societies Heading? 183

Notes 196

Index 217

Introduction

BERNIE SANDERS AND OTHER LEFTIST politicians want to increase taxes, regulate businesses, and create a society where government takes responsibility for many aspects of daily life. If you are sick, the public sector should pay for your treatment and give you sick leave benefits. If you quit your job, taxpayers should support you. If you have a low income, the government should transfer money from your neighbor who has a better job. While many believe that the public sector should provide some help in these situations, there are those on the left who believe that nearly all the responsibility should be on the public sector and little on the individual, families, and other parts of civil society. The ideal is a society in which the state makes sure that those who work and those who don't have a similar living standard. There is nothing odd about these views. They are classical socialist ideas, or as Bernie Sanders himself would explain, the core ideas of social democracy.

These days, few people believe in pure socialism. The system has failed, leading to human misery on a wide scale in every country in which it has been introduced. The Soviet Union, Cuba, Venezuela, and North Korea are hardly positive role models. China, the last major socialist country, has in many ways transitioned to a capitalist economy. A less radical idea that is gaining ground is social democracy. Contrary to socialism, social democracy isn't meant to be introduced through an authoritarian system where one party monopolizes power. It is to be combined with democracy and also the free market. In social democracy government takes control of some, but not all, parts of the economy within the frame of a democratic system. Services such as education, health care, and elderly care are provided through public monopolies, and funded by tax money.

> "I think we should look to countries like Denmark, like Sweden and Norway and learn from what they have accomplished for their working people." —BERNIE SANDERS, 2015

Social democracy is becoming increasingly popular among the Left in the United States. An important reason is that positive role models exist. In fact, a number of countries with social democratic policies—namely, the Nordic nations—have seemingly become everything that the Left would like America to be: prosperous, yet equal and with good social outcomes. Bernie Sanders himself has explained: "I think we should look to countries like Denmark, like Sweden and Norway and learn from what they have accomplished for their working people."[1]

I fully understand the Left's admiration for the Nordic countries. In 1989 I emigrated with my family from Iran to Sweden and grew up in a typical immigrant household, supported mainly by welfare benefits. I graduated, got my PhD, and started writing about politics. Since then I have written more than a hundred policy reports and some twenty books about various societal issues in Sweden and other northern European countries. This part of the world has indeed fascinating social systems. It is true, as Bernie Sanders and his supporters say, that the Nordic welfare states provide a host of benefits. To give an example from my own upbringing, taxpayers fully paid for my higher education, affording opportunities to a person from one of the poorer households in society.

What is less known on the other side of the Atlantic is that the Nordic welfare states also create a range of social problems. An example from my own upbringing is that many of my friends, although bright, never studied or got a meaningful job. My best friend started a criminal gang. This is not just my personal experience, but sadly it is a common fate of many migrants to Sweden. I am sure that this might sound odd for American admirers of social democracy. If the government provides generous benefits, even fully funded higher education, shouldn't more people be lifted out of poverty? The reality is that Nordic policies trap many families, particularly those with an immigrant background, in welfare dependency. This is why, as I show in detail later in this book, the American Dream of income mobility is more vivid in capitalist America than in the Nordic welfare state systems.

If people such as Bernie Sanders were truly interested in

learning from the Nordic experience, I am sure they could expand their horizon. The pragmatic Nordic people have created relatively well-functioning public sectors, in contrast to the less efficient bureaucracy that exists in America. The Nordic welfare states certainly have their advantages. Public provision of child care, for example, allows many women to work. A closer look at the systems, however, shatters the rosy illusion of the Left. The welfare states of the north are dealing with challenges stemming from the long-term effects of high taxes, generous benefits, and public-sector monopolies. From Spain to the Baltics, Latin America and the United States, leftist ideologues hedge much of their political beliefs on the success of Nordic social democracy. In the Nordics themselves, this ideal image of democratic socialism has lost its shimmer.

> Leftist ideologues hedge much of their political beliefs on the success of Nordic social democracy. In the Nordics themselves, this ideal image of democratic socialism has lost its shimmer.

It is possible that social democracy will again become popular in the Nordics. For the last decades, however, the labor movement and the Social Democratic parties have gradually lost support, and shifted considerably toward the right. As a simple illustration, let's look at the current governments in the Nordics. Denmark, the Nordic country with the highest tax burden in the world (taxes correspond to about 50 percent of the Danish economy, nearly twice the rate as in the United States), is led by Lars Løkke Rasmussen. The prime minister holds together a coalition of center-right parties. The previous government was led by the Social Democrats, who—I am sure this would shock leftist ideologues in the United States if they knew—during their term openly challenged the idea of a generous welfare system, and explained that Denmark needed a new system with more emphasis on individual responsibility. While it is true that Denmark has high taxes and a large public sector, the country has embraced capitalism in virtually every other way. The *Index of Economic Freedom*, compiled by the American think tank the Heritage Foundation in partnership with the *Wall Street Journal*, ranks Denmark as the twelfth most economically free country in the world. This is just one step after the United States.[2]

Finland is also ruled by a center-right coalition. The prime minister is previous businessman Juha Petri Sipilä, who has quite a conservative stand on the issue of immigration. Sigmundur Davíð Gunnlaugsson, the prime minister of Iceland, is yet again the head of a center-right coalition. Free-market and small-government ideas have become quite popular in Iceland, a country that never fully embraced Nordic-style democratic socialism. Norway is led by conservative party leader Erna Solberg. The massive oil wealth of Norway would make a generous welfare state more feasible than elsewhere. Over time, however, even Norwegians have been alarmed over how working ethics are eroded by a system where much responsibility is placed on the public sector and little on the individual.

An issue that has come to dominate the Nordic political landscape is that of immigration. At the end of this book, I will describe more in detail how the welfare systems in this part of the world are much less successful than America's when it comes to integrating immigrants. This explains in part why voters in the Nordic countries have turned to anti-immigration parties, which often have a socially conservative stance and are seen by their adversaries as populists, not unlike Donald Trump's position in the American presidential cycle. The Norwegian prime minister's government is described as a Blue-Blue Cabinet, since it is a two-party minority government consisting of the Conservative Party and the anti-immigration Progress Party.[3] In Finland the anti-immigration Finns Party is part of the government, while in Denmark the anti-immigrant Danish People's Party supports the current government. Iceland's two largest parties are both skeptical of the European Union, and the public opinion in the country is overall against open borders. To sum up, conservative parties are in power in most Nordic nations, while anti-immigration parties with a populist touch have been gaining ground. This political landscape is far from what is favored by liberals in the United States, although few American admirers of Nordic-style democratic socialism seem aware of this.

As this book is being written, only one of five Nordic countries has a social democratic government. That country is Sweden, where the previous center-right government implemented significant tax reductions, opened up public monopolies, and limited the generosity of the welfare state. One might have expected a major leftist backlash to these reforms. However, the Left didn't come to power in late 2014 because they increased their support (the three parties on the left only gained 0.2

percent more votes than in the previous election), but rather because the anti-immigration party, the Sweden Democrats, took many votes from the center-right parties. The party, which also attracts many traditional social democrat voters, had previously minimal support due to its neo-Nazi origins.

Marco Rubio joked during a Fox News debate among Republican presidential candidates, "I think Bernie Sanders is a good candidate for president—of Sweden."[4] While the audience laughed, Swedish royalist Roger Lundgren remarked that the country has a king and prime minister, no president. More important, the Sanders brand of socialism is not particularly popular these days in Sweden. For much of the twentieth century, the Social Democrats in Sweden were seen as a one-party state, with support from half the population. As shown in the image on the next page, however, voter support for Social Democrats and Socialists has fallen significantly over time.[5]

The political debate in the Nordics is not much different from that in the United States. As I am writing these words, one of the major issues being discussed in Sweden is how high-entry-level wages are creating unemployment. This is similar to the American debate about minimum wages, with the only difference being that Sweden doesn't have any minimum wage legislation. Another urgent topic is how a massive shortage of housing has resulted from rent control and burdensome regulation. A third one is how more and more people are relying on sick leave benefits. Sweden doesn't seem to have a major epidemic going on, but rather a situation where people are increasingly taking advantage of the generous sick leave insurance system. And lastly, one issue dwarfs all others in the Swedish debate: how can the cost of immigration be curbed and how can the social challenges relating to immigration be dealt with?

Integrating immigrants on the labour market is a challenge for most modern economies, not least when it comes to those who come from countries with poor education systems. And it is certainly no news that the generous welfare state models in northern Europe are particularly bad at integration, since their systems trap many families in long-term welfare dependency. As these words are being written, Swedish politicians are conducting a rather ill-fated experiment where extremely progressive welfare state ideas are being combined with open borders. The results are, as discussed in the end of this book, anything but encouraging. The Swedish welfare state is not, as some wrongly claim, collapsing under the weight of immigration. But it is certainly being strained. To give a short example, in 2015 so many immigrants arrived in the southern part of the country that all available mattresses were reportedly sold out.[6] Sweden's third largest city, Malmö, which is located in the south, is struggling with social tension and falling school results. Grenades being thrown in the streets of Malmö by rival gangs—once thought unimaginable in peaceful Sweden—are now part of everyday life. One-fifth of the social service workers in the city reportedly quit their jobs in 2015 while fully half of those that remained signed off due to illness, since they were so stressed in their working environment.[7]

Part of these challenges are surely temporary and relate to the open door immigration policies, which abruptly ended in late 2015. And much of them—such as the dramatically falling school results in Sweden—have more to do with the failing of progressive policies than with immigration. As late as 1985 the Social Democrats and their Socialist supporters gained a majority of the votes in Sweden. In the two recent elections they have only received a little more than a third of votes. As of early February 2016, the Social Democrats had never polled so low in modern history. A poll of polls by Swedish magazine *Dagens Samhälle* shows that less than a third of voters are backing either the Social Democrats or the Socialists. Without the support of the Green party, which is careful in not identifying itself as socialist, the Swedish Left would find it difficult to gain power.[8] Jonas Hinnfors, professor in social sciences, is one among many experts who has commented on the crisis of Swedish Social Democrats. According to Hinnfors, the party suffers from a long-term and deep sense of disorientation.[9]

More to the point, it is doubtful if Sanders would even be welcome in the Swedish Social Democrats, who are fiscally conservative. When the socialist vote was strong in the 1970s, the Social Democrats would really identify themselves as socialists. At the same time the Socialists were a communist party that dreamed of a violent revolution and took orders from the Soviet regime in Moscow. Today, Sweden's Social Democrats position themselves more as centrists, not unlike Hillary Clinton, while even the Socialists have to some point embraced the market.[10] It remains to be seen if the Nordic Social Democrats can reinvent themselves or not. My guess is that they will, by further turning away from socialism to pragmatic centrism.

The global Left doesn't understand that a unique culture underlies the success in Nordic countries.

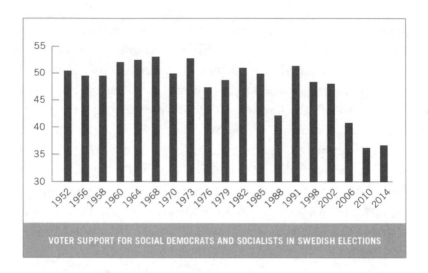

VOTER SUPPORT FOR SOCIAL DEMOCRATS AND SOCIALISTS IN SWEDISH ELECTIONS

It might seem odd that Nordic-style democratic socialism is all the rage among leftist ideologues in other countries, but to a large degree is rejected by the people in the Nordic countries themselves. If we take a closer look, we find that this apparent paradox has a simple explanation: the global Left doesn't understand that a unique culture underlies the success in Nordic countries. Therefore, ideologues vastly exaggerate the benefits of the social systems in these countries. During the past years I have written a number of articles and longer publications dealing with this Nordic utopian image. My arguments, in short, are these:

- Yes, it is true that Nordic people have longer life expectancies than in most other countries. But no, this isn't simply the proof that large welfare states with universal health care extend the life span. Before the Nordic countries introduced large welfare states, the difference in life span compared to the average American's was even larger than today. Iceland, the Nordic country which has the smallest welfare state, has seen the most significant increase in life expectancy during recent years. The main reason for the difference in life expectancy is obviously culture. Nordic people have healthy lifestyles and diets, which explains why they live so long.

- Yes, it is true that Nordic countries are rich and have high taxes. But this doesn't prove that high taxes lead to prosperity. In fact, study after study has shown that the affluent Nordic economies would be even more successful if they had lower taxes. There are few places in the world where the negative effects of taxation have been so well documented as in Sweden and Denmark, the two Nordic countries with the highest tax burdens. Sweden has moved toward significant tax reductions, while Denmark compensates for its high taxes by being very market friendly in other areas.

- Yes, it is true that Nordic people have low levels of poverty. And certainly, to some degree we can explain this by the aid given to the less fortunate by the public sector. However, researchers have convincingly shown that Nordic countries moved toward income equality in a time when they combined small public sectors and low taxes with free markets. Another observation is that simply adopting Nordic-style welfare states does not remove poverty, as has been the experience in France, Italy, Spain, and other parts of Europe.

- We know that many immigrants in the Nordic countries struggle to get a job and otherwise be included in society. If anything, they are trapped in poverty and dependency on public handouts. The lack of upward mobility for immigrants is a telling sign that there are limits to the success of the Nordic welfare model. Sweden, which has been more open to immigration than its Nordic neighbors, is currently experiencing a massive increase in inequality.[11] Both high-educated and low-educated people of foreign origin have greater success in finding a job in America than in the Nordics.

An obvious explanation for all this is culture. Over centuries Nordic societies have relied on a particularly strong brand of Protestant working ethics. These stoic societies put great emphasis on hard work, individual responsibility, sobriety, and education. For this very same reason, the people of Nordic origin whose forefathers have migrated to the United States are today prospering. They have the same or even lower poverty levels than their cousins in the Nordics, although living in the capitalist American system that Bernie Sanders and other ideologues on the left are convinced is the root of social ills.

During the summer of 2015, I published the short book *Scandinavian Unexceptionalism: Culture, Markets and the Failure of Third-Way Socialism* for the Institute of Economic Affairs, a London-based think tank.[12] The research-oriented book summarized the arguments above, taking quite some inspiration from the ideas of my brother, Tino Sanandaji—an economist from the University of Chicago who is currently doing research on the Stockholm School of Economics and teaching classes at the University of Cambridge. Tino has discovered many groundbreaking insights into the connection between culture, economy, and social development, and has aided me in my writings. *Scandinavian Unexceptionalism* quickly gained media attention around the world. The book and my previous writings on the subject have already been translated into a number of languages, including Spanish, Farsi, Polish, and Korean.

I am very glad that WND Books has given me the opportunity to write this book, aimed at an American audience, about the lessons we can learn from Nordic welfare states. I know that it is mainly conservatives and libertarians who have shown interest in my ideas, seeing them as a way of debunking the favorite arguments of leftist ideologues and politicians such as Bernie Sanders. And certainly, this book will burst many popular leftist myths. It will also argue that the Nordic experience, perhaps more than anywhere else in the world, teaches us about the benefits of free markets and traditional values, such as a strong work ethic and individual responsibility. However, my point is not to criticize Nordic welfare states head-on or to simply write an ideological pamphlet for the Right. Rather, if we set rosy, idealistic views aside and take an in-depth look at countries such as Sweden, Denmark, Norway, Finland, and Iceland, we can learn about both the shortcomings and the successes of welfare-state programs. The world isn't black or white. And the Nordic welfare states—for all the turmoil they have been experiencing lately—can still teach us much, at least for those interested in a more nuanced view. According to a traditional Persian saying, you can learn at least as much from the mistakes of others as from their successes. In the case of the Nordics, we should learn from both.

Part 1

THE NORDIC SHANGRI-LA

1

AMERICAN OBSESSION WITH NORDIC

SOCIAL DEMOCRACY

DURING THE 2016 DEMOCRATIC PRIMARY, Bernie Sanders has repeatedly claimed that the Nordic welfare systems are role models for the United States to follow.[1] Already in 2013 Sanders wrote extensively on this point, with reference to a meeting with the Danish ambassador. Among others Sanders explained:

> In Denmark, social policy in areas like health care, child care, education and protecting the unemployed are part of a "solidarity system" that makes sure that almost no one falls into economic despair. Danes pay very high taxes, but in return enjoy a quality of life that many Americans would find hard to believe. . . .
>
> In Denmark, there is a very different understanding of what "freedom" means. In that country, they have gone a long way to ending the enormous anxieties that comes with economic insecurity. Instead of promoting a system which allows a few to have enormous wealth, they have developed a system which guarantees

a strong minimal standard of living to all—including the children, the elderly and the disabled.[2]

By pointing to Nordic social democracy as a role model, ideologues on the left can create optimism for the progressive cause in America.

The admiration of Nordic social democracy seems to resonate with liberal grassroots, which in turn can explain why Sanders has been able to compete with the much more established, and better funded, candidate Hillary Clinton. This really doesn't come as a surprise. By pointing to Nordic social democracy as a role model, ideologues on the left can create optimism for the progressive cause in America. They point out that the Nordic model allows for universal health care, fully government-funded education, a system where most workers are part of labor unions, generous parental leave, open-handed unemployment benefits, liberal sick leave benefits and a lavish system with paid vacations. What more could the Left in the United States ask for? Hillary Clinton has tried to position herself in the middle, by combining praise of the Nordic model with a less enthusiastic stand on how far the United States should go in pursuit of democratic socialism. In her own words: "We are not Denmark. I love Denmark. We are the United States of America, and it is our job to rein in the excesses of capitalism." Ezra Klein, editor of the liberal news website Vox, explained that this dispute "obscured deep similarities," as "Clinton and Sanders both want to make America look a lot more like Denmark—they both want to pass generous parental leave policies, let the government bargain down drug prices, and strengthen the social safety net. Their disagreement isn't over whether America should look more like Denmark."[3]

Hillary and Bill Clinton for their part are also associated to the Nordic countries in the 2016 election cycle. The primary reason is a scandal, where the Clintons are accused of having set up and kept hidden a foundation in Sweden, which has received $26 million, with one of the main contributors being a Swedish government–sanctioned lottery.[4] The Clintons also have ideological ties to the Nordics. Although the two centrist Democrats are careful not to identify themselves as admirers of democratic socialism, they too lean towards the Nordic model. In 1997, for example, Bill Clinton became the first sitting president to visit Denmark. Clinton, who had visited the country already during 1969 as a student, praised Danish policies, saying, "Denmark has been a pioneer in showing the world how a nation can succeed, both in creating a strong economy and a good society that provides opportunity for all its citizens and supports those in need, a society bound together by shared values and respect for real differences. We can all learn from your efforts to educate your people for a lifetime, to give them the tools necessary to make the most of their own lives in a time of global, economic, and technological change."[5] In his book *Back to Work*, published in 2011, Bill Clinton went further by explaining that Finland, Sweden, and Norway offer more chances for individuals to out-earn their parents than the United States does.[6]

Obama is fond of musing to his aides, "Why can't all countries

be like the Nordic countries?"—CNN, 2016

In 2013 Obama followed suit by making the first bilateral visit by an American president to Sweden. After a joint speech with Sweden's then prime minister Fredrik Reinfeldt, Obama explained that he admired Sweden's economic model: "Sweden also has been able to have a robust market economy while recognizing that there are some investments in education or infrastructure or research that are important, and there's no contradiction between making public investments and being a firm believer in free markets. And that's a debate and a discussion that we often have in the United States."[7]

Three years later, in May 2016, Obama hosted the leaders of the Nordic countries in Washington. He continued to praise the Nordic social welfare model, and the open immigration policies of the Nordics. Amongst others Obama said: "We believe in societies that create opportunity for all people, through education, health care, and equal opportunity—including for women. In fact, in a world of growing economic disparities, Nordic countries have some of the least income inequality in the world—which may explain one of the reasons that they're some of the happiest people in the world, despite not getting much sun. . . . There have been times where I've said, why don't we just put all these small countries in charge for a while? And they could clean things up." In a story for CNN White House producer Kevin Liptak explained "the northern European nations remain an oasis of liberal cool for [Obama] . . . It's no wonder

Obama is fond of musing to his aides, 'Why can't all countries be like the Nordic countries?'"[8]

The admiration shown by Democrat presidents or would-be presidents is however only the tip of the iceberg. For a long time the Nordic countries have been regarded as prime role models by leftist ideologues. I don't know of any part of the world in which the Left does not view the Nordics as examples of how high-tax social democratic systems are viable and successful. American musician Bruce Springsteen, famous for getting engaged in politics, explained during a tour in Paris that his dream was for the United States to adopt a Swedish-style welfare state.[9] He is joined by many liberal intellectuals and journalists who over decades have built up the image of the nearly perfect Nordics. *Time* magazine, for example, described Sweden as a social democratic utopia already in 1976, going as far as using the word *paradise*: "It is a country whose very name has become a synonym for a materialist paradise. Its citizens enjoy one of the world's highest living standards, and a great many possess symbols of individual affluence: a private home or a modern apartment, a family car, a *stuga* (summer cottage) and often a sailboat. No slums disfigure their cities, their air and water are largely pollution-free, and they have ever more leisure to indulge a collective passion for being *ut i naturen* (out in nature) in their half-forested country. Neither ill health, unemployment nor old age pose the terror of financial hardship."[10]

Do you oppose creating a paradise of wealth and equality? Are you against having a society where no one needs to be financially worried when they are sick, out of a job, or old? Well, who can be? The American Left has created a utopian image of Sweden in particular and the Nordic countries in general. Based on this unrealistic image, they argue that social democracy is superior to a free-market model. Political scientist John Logue stated in 1979, "A simple visual comparison of Scandinavian towns with American equivalents provides strong evidence that reasonably efficient welfare measures can abolish poverty as it was known in the past; economic growth alone, as the American case indicates, does not."[11] Logue believed that the greatest threat to the Nordic welfare states was that they were too successful; eliminating social problems to such a degree that people forgot the importance of welfare policies.[12]

In 1994 David Popenoe wrote that "Scandinavian welfare and family policies are the envy of [left] liberal-thinking people around the world." He, "like most American social researchers," was "largely in support of the Scandinavians' accomplishments in the area of social welfare."[13] It might not seem like it, but Popenoe was actually trying to burst the utopian bubble by explaining that there were indeed also drawbacks to the generous welfare systems supported by high taxes. The bubble, however, did not burst, even among top leftist academics. In 2006 Jeffrey Sachs, one of the world's leading experts on economic development and the fight against poverty, argued in *Scientific American* that the ideas of free-market economist Friedrich Hayek were proven wrong by the Nordic social democracies: "In strong and vibrant democracies, a generous social-welfare state is not a road to serfdom but rather to fairness, economic equality and international competitiveness."[14] In 2011 liberal American economic guru Paul Krugman explained, "Every time I read someone talking about the 'collapsing welfare states of Europe,' I have this urge to take that person on a forced walking tour of Stockholm."[15] Journalists with a tilt to the left also add to the equation. During the presidential campaign of 2016, Hillary Clinton was criticized, among others in the *Boston Globe*, for not being enough of an admirer of the Nordic model.[16]

> "Every time I read someone talking about the 'collapsing welfare states of Europe,' I have this urge to take that person on a forced walking tour of Stockholm." —LIBERAL ECONOMIC GURU PAUL KRUGMAN

This list of admirers could be easily extended. Also in other parts of the world, the Nordic model is routinely seen as a great system to follow. I think this is the simple explanation for why my previous writings on this issue have gained so much attention abroad. Again, it would be one thing if people argued in a nuanced way in favor of the welfare states. I myself don't believe that universal health care or public funding of child care and schooling is a bad idea. As I will explain in this book, one could certainly make a case for the early Nordic model, where low taxes and market-friendly policies were combined with such basic welfare services. Admirers of the Nordic system, however, often go all in, in the utopian myth creation. The leading French newspaper *Le Monde* has, for example, explained that "only the Scandinavian system is at once efficient and fair."[17]

Rich Lowry, editor of the right-leaning *National Review*, recently used Shangri-La as an analogue for the American Left's view of Nordic welfare states, in an article on Scandinavian unexceptionalism. I think this is a spot-on description, at least for the most vivid foreign advocates of Nordic-style social democracy.[18]

The high regard among the admirers of welfare state policy around the world, from Asia to Europe to Latin America, comes as no surprise. Nordic societies are uniquely successful. They characterized not only by high living standards, but also by other attractive features, such as low crime rates, long life expectations, high degrees of social cohesion, and even income distributions. Various international rankings conclude that they are among the best, if not the best, places in the world in which to live. One example is the Better Life Index, compiled by the Organization for Economic Cooperation and Development (OECD). In the 2015 edition of the index, Sweden was ranked as the nation with the second-highest level of well-being in the world. The other four Nordic countries also made the top ten global list (see next page).[19] Another example is the 2015 edition of Mothers' Index Rankings, where Save the Children rates nations based on how favorable their social and economic systems are for mothers and children. Norway ranks as the best country in the world in this regard, followed by Finland, Iceland, Denmark, and Sweden.[20] The Nordics have been on top in previous years also.

If one disregards the importance of thinking carefully about causality, the argument for adopting a Scandinavian-style economic policy in other nations seems obvious. The Nordic nations—in particular, Sweden, which is most often used as an international role model—have large welfare states and are successful. This is often seen as proof that a third-way policy between socialism and capitalism works well, and that other societies can reach the same favorable social outcomes simply by expanding the size of government. If one studies Nordic history and society in depth, however, it quickly becomes evident that the simplistic analysis is flawed. The social success of Nordic countries is, as will be shown systematically throughout this book, rooted deeply in their history and was apparent long before the adaptation of large welfare states. Although welfare states certainly provide some benefits, to a large degree much-admired societies in the north are successful despite, not thanks to, their policies.

TOP TEN COUNTRIES: OECD BETTER LIFE INDEX 2015

1.	Australia		6.	Canada
2.	Sweden		7.	United States
3.	Norway		8.	New Zealand
4.	Switzerland		9.	Iceland
5.	Denmark		10.	Finland

Source: OECD Better Life Index

2

NORDIC SUCCESS PREDATES LARGE
WELFARE STATES

DEMOCRATIC PRESIDENTS AND WOULD-BE PRESIDENTS, liberal academics, journalists, and Hollywood celebrities who admire Nordic social democracy all make a simple assumption: if America adopts Nordic policies, American society will shape into a Nordic society. To paraphrase the movie *Field of Dreams,* "If you build it, he will come."[1] But does this assumption make sense? Italy, France, and Greece also have high government expenditure and welfare states based on socialist ambitions. Why wouldn't America turn out to be the next Greece, Italy, or France? I am sure there is a point to be made about the benefits of generous welfare systems in these countries. At the same time, it is obvious that social challenges such as unrest, high unemployment, and stagnant growth exist in southern European welfare states. They are far from the Nordic Shangri-La.

Ideologues on the left often simply avoid this question. Bernie Sanders isn't keen on comparing his policies with those introduced by socialists in southern Europe, although his ideals are arguably more popular there today than in the Nordics. Southern European social democrats have a lax attitude about public spending, while those in northern Europe are fiscally conservative. Which of the two reminds you more of the attitudes of American politicians who want to introduce social democracy? There is also the issue of outcomes. When you think about it, have states in America that have moved toward social democratic policies, such as California, been able to replicate the success of Nordic societies? Or have their outcomes been more in line with the welfare states of southern Europe? Again, the point isn't to dismiss the idea of welfare programs, but to have realistic expectations on the limits of policy.

To understand the Nordic experience, bear in mind that the large welfare states are not the only thing that sets these countries apart from the rest of the world. The countries also have homogenous populations with nongovernmental social institutions that are uniquely adapted to the modern world. High levels of trust, a strong work ethic, civic participation, social cohesion, individual responsibility, and family values are long-standing features of Nordic society that predate the welfare state. These deeper social institutions explain much of the success in the Nordics. Serious researchers of course understand what ideologues often neglect. One example is Danish scholar Henrik Jacobsen Kleven, a professor at the London School of Economics. In a paper he explains:

> As we continue our efforts to understand and draw lessons from the social and economic success of the Scandinavian countries, it is worth remembering that these countries have some specific traits.

They are small and homogenous, racial and religious diversity is limited, human capital is high, and they have been largely unaffected by violent conflict. It is not clear to what degree lessons learned from Scandinavia carry policy implications for large, diverse, and unequal countries such as the United States. Certainly the political economy surrounding the implementation of the policies proposed here would be different in the United States—indeed this is partly why we observe stark policy differences to begin with—and conditional on political feasibility, the effects and appropriate design of those policies might be different in the United States. Hence, replicating the Scandinavian policies and institutions in societies that are fundamentally different is unlikely to be achievable or perhaps even desirable.[2]

In other words, the Nordic countries' unique cultural and historical attributes explain why they are successful. Therefore, it is wrong to assume that adapting a large Nordic welfare state would turn the United States into a Nordic society. The author also hints that one reason why the Nordic countries have adopted different policies than the United States might be precisely because their historic and cultural attributes make them more suited to large welfare states. It makes sense, doesn't it? If you have homogenous societies with strong working ethics, healthy lifestyles, and high levels of trust it is more feasible to introduce a generous welfare system than if you have heterogeneous societies where a significant part of the population, to give just one example, have unhealthy lifestyles and therefore create high costs for universal health care. Of course, the United States can introduce a Nordic-style social democratic model, but we shouldn't expect this to be as successful as in the Nordics.

The next part of this book will explain the origins of this unique culture of success, and how it allows Nordic Americans to be at least as affluent and socially successful as their cousins in the Nordics. This chapter will make two simple, but striking, points. The first is that the success of the Nordic welfare state, much admired by the Left in America and elsewhere, predates the welfare state. The Nordic countries became economically and socially successful before they transitioned to large welfare states. A historic view shatters the utopian illusion of how successful social democracy has been in the Nordics. The second point is that social and economic success is indeed concentrated to northern Europe, but not necessarily to countries with socialist policies.

Take Switzerland, as an example. In chapter 1 we learned that Switzerland has the fourth-highest level of well-being in the world, according to the OECD Better Life Index. In some areas, such as employment rate and living standard, Switzerland out-performs the Nordic nations. Switzerland has a similar culture and climate to the Nordic nations, but vastly different policies. It is a conservative country both culturally and economically. The Swiss system stresses individual responsibility, strong families, and a competitive market economy rather than a large welfare state. This of course has both merits and disadvantages. One thing we can observe is that Switzerland is achieving much of the social success that the Left admires. Why shouldn't America be more like Switzerland? Why not, for that matter, Australia, which according to the same index has the highest well-being in the world? Australia also has market-oriented policies and a small welfare state.

It is also worth comparing Iceland with the other Nordic societies. The isolated island, which was populated by Viking sailors in the late ninth century, has arguably the most uniquely Nordic culture in the world. Yet it has never embraced large welfare states to the same extent as its larger cousins. Iceland certainly faces many challenges: it is far from other places, has too small a population to create a specialized economy, most of its lands are inhabitable, and, well, it is covered with ice. Large parts of its surface are barren and unfruitful. Sure, Iceland has geothermal energy, but it has few mineral resources and lacks the oil wealth of places such as Norway and Alaska. Still, as this chapter will demonstrate, the country is in many ways as successful, sometimes even more, as its cousins with larger welfare states. Given all its disadvantages, for example, Iceland is only a little less affluent than its Nordic cousins, even somewhat ahead of Finland.[3]

An interesting fact about the Nordics that is seldom acknowledged by the admirers of social democracy is that the countries have not always had large welfare states. Welfare state institutions such as public schooling were gradually introduced in the late nineteenth century and the first half of the twentieth century. The extent of welfare policies was, however, not exceptional. Instead it was in line with the introduction of similar policies in other parts of Europe, and for that matter, in the United States. The common measure of the size of government is how much of the total economy—that is to say, the gross domestic product (GDP)—goes to taxes. By looking at this measure, we can conclude that the size of government was about the same in the Nordic countries as in the United Stated during the mid-twentieth century. The point where policies started to differ is somewhere around 1960. At this time point the size of government was similar in the Nordics to the United States, while afterwards the Nordics gradually built up a larger public sector, funded by higher taxes.[4]

So we have established a year when the taxes in the Nordics were still relatively low, 1960. Let's also establish another year, when the Nordic welfare states were at their peak. This occurred somewhere around the year 2000. At this time taxes in the United States had remained on about the same level as in 1960, while those in the Nordics had nearly doubled to close to half of GDP. Since then at least Sweden has substantially reduced its tax burden and the scope of the welfare state.[5] By comparing 1960 to 2000, we can see how much of the social achievements of the Nordics came before and after the shift toward big government. It is, of course, also interesting to look at the present situation. So what do we find if we look at some broad measures of social success?

LONG LIFE SPANS DUE TO LARGE WELFARE STATES?

In late 2015, the Public Broadcasting Service (PBS) ran a story entitled "What Can the U.S. Learn from Denmark?" by the Associated Press. The AP explained, "Danes were excited this week to see their calm and prosperous country thrust into the spotlight of the U.S. presidential race when Democratic hopefuls Bernie Sanders and Hillary Clinton sparred over whether there's something Americans can learn from Denmark's social model." The story continued by stating that "Danes get free or heavily subsidized health care" and "compensation when they're unemployed, out sick from work or on parental leave." Additionally, they have longer life spans than Americans.[6] Now, all these statements are certainly true. The only problem is that many assume that these facts are directly correlated. Danes have universal health care and government compensation when sick. Correspondingly they live longer than Americans. So, for the United States to raise its life expectancy, perhaps a Danish model should be adopted? After all, what kind of heartless monster would you be to oppose policies that increase people's life spans?

I am myself in favor of the public sector providing health care, and for that matter, sick leave compensations, particularly to the less well off. But the simplistic comparison troubles me. As it turns out, according to the latest available data, Danes have on average 1.5 years longer life expectancy than Americans.[7] However, during 1960, when the country actually had slightly lower taxes than the United States (27 percent in the United States compared to 25 percent in Denmark),[8] the difference was even larger. At this time Danes lived 2.4 years longer than Americans.[9] How many admirers of the Danish high tax model are aware that the shift toward massive taxation and a correspondingly generous welfare state has led to a smaller difference in life expectancy than before? How many are even aware that Denmark used to have lower taxes than the United States?

Interestingly, Denmark is not alone in this regard. When Nordic countries had similarly sized public sectors as the United States (1960), Swedes lived 3.2 years longer than Americans while Norwegians lived 3.8 years longer. Today the difference has shrunk to 2.9 years in Sweden and 2.6 years in Norway. This analysis isn't sensitive to what exact year we choose. Finland, a war-torn and poor country at the time, had one year's lower life expectancy than the United States and has now almost two years longer, since it has caught up with its Nordic cousins. Iceland is even more interesting. Icelanders went from having 3.7 years' longer life span than Americans in 1960 to 4.3 years longer today. So, does this fit in with the idea that large welfare states promote long life spans? Well, let's not forget that Iceland is the Nordic country that, over time, has had the *smallest* welfare state, with least leaning toward social democracy.

Instead of solely comparing with the United States, let's compare with the world. The table on the next page shows the top ten countries with the longest life spans during three periods. In 1960, when the Nordics had small welfare states, Norway had the highest life expectancy in the world, followed by Iceland in second place, and Sweden and Denmark in fourth and fifth. In 2000, during the peak of the Nordic welfare states, Norway and Denmark had dropped out of the top-ten league. Sweden had fallen to tenth place and Iceland to fourth. The latest data shows a similar picture, except that Iceland has again climbed to second position. Pretty interesting, huh? Just for the sake of curiosity, do we find in general that countries with large welfare states have the longest life spans today? We do not. Japan, which currently has the highest life span, has conservative, family-oriented policies and relatively low taxes. The same is true for Switzerland, which has the third-highest life span; Singapore, which has the fifth highest; and Australia, which has the seventh highest. Instead of politics, the common feature seems to be that these are countries where people eat healthily and exercise. Perhaps this shows that systems that put emphasis on big welfare states as well as systems that put emphasis on market economy, individual responsibility, and family-oriented policies can achieve long life spans. Or perhaps it shows that politics cannot fully solve our problems. Social outcomes are to a large extent determined by the choices that people make, which in turn is influenced by culture. A country cannot just copy the policies of another country and hope to gain the same social outcomes.

TOP TEN COUNTRIES WITH LONGEST LIFE SPAN

1960 (SMALL PUBLIC SECTORS IN NORDICS)	2000 (PEAK OF NORDIC WELFARE STATES)	2013 (LATEST DATA)
NORWAY	JAPAN	JAPAN
ICELAND	SWITZERLAND	ICELAND
NETHERLANDS	ITALY	SWITZERLAND
SWEDEN	ICELAND	SPAIN
DENMARK	AUSTRALIA	SINGAPORE
SWITZERLAND	FRANCE	ITALY
NEW ZEALAND	SPAIN	AUSTRALIA
CANADA	ISRAEL	ISRAEL
UNITED KINGDOM	SINGAPORE	FRANCE
AUSTRALIA	SWEDEN	SWEDEN

Source: World Bank World Development Indicators Database.
Microstates have been excluded.

Long Nordic life expectancy is anything but a mystery. Much as in 1960, the populations in this part of the world combine healthy diets with a love of nature and sports. The Icelandic people do live in a cold country, with large, barren, volcanic fields that resemble the fictional Mordor from *Lord of the Rings*, yet, they enjoy going out in this nature. Also, they eat a healthy diet based largely on fish. That Denmark has fallen out of the global top-ten list in life expectancy doesn't come as a surprise either. It is not because Danes have such a well-funded universal health care sector that they say, "The hell with it; let's live unhealthy lives." The explanation lies in culture. The Danes are famous for enjoying life more than their Nordic cousins. This goes hand in hand with high rates of alcohol consumption and smoking.

Certainly, having some sort of system where people who are sick are given treatment is vital for public health. Preventive health care interventions by the welfare state—for example, where individuals at risk of future health problems are identified and encouraged to change their diets and lifestyles—can have great effects. But large welfare simply doesn't translate to high life expectancy. If that were the case, Danes would live longer than Swedes, who in turn would live longer than Icelanders. The opposite is true. Once we realize this, perhaps American admirers of the Nordic model should change their perspective: Instead of trying to copy Nordic policies, why not copy their healthy lifestyles? Wouldn't Americans be healthier if they exercised more, took hikes in nature, walked to the store on occasion (as Nordic people often do) instead of driving, and ate less junk food and more fish? If anything, isn't it remarkable that the difference in life span is so small—and has shrunk over time—given that Americans have much less healthy lifestyles? Perhaps some Americans would like to continue having an unsound diet and hope that Nordic-style social democracy can improve their health. I very much doubt that would be the case.

LOW CHILD MORTALITY DUE TO LARGE WELFARE STATES?
Besides life span, another common measure of how well societies are doing is child mortality. The levels of child mortality basically tell us three things:

- how good and how widely available health care is for mothers;

- how many parents go to the hospital to give birth rather than stay home; and

- what share of mothers have issues such as alcoholism, smoking, and drug abuse, which could seriously hurt their infants.

Much like life expectancy, the United States doesn't come on top on this indicator.

The child mortality rate in America is 5.6 among 1,000 children. This is twice the rate in Denmark and Sweden, three times that of Norway and Finland, and nearly four times that of Iceland.[10] Again, the simple argument could be: "In America more than twice as many children die at a young age as in the Nordics. Therefore, if you aren't in favor of Nordic-style social democracy, you don't want to protect children." Now, perhaps Americans could learn a thing or two from Nordic maternal care. But isn't the obvious problem the poverty, and related addiction to alcohol and drugs, which exists in particular among marginalized minorities in the United States? One could of course argue that poverty would vanish if a larger welfare system existed in America. But where is the proof? Have states with higher taxes significantly reduced social ills? Why not?

Again, we can turn to a global analysis. The following table shows the top ten countries with the lowest child mortality at different times. We can see that the five Nordic countries all have among the lowest child mortalities in the world today. The same situation existed during the peak of welfare policy and when Nordic countries had the same low taxes as in the United States. Over time Denmark and Sweden, the two Nordic countries with the highest tax burden, fall behind somewhat, while Iceland goes from third to first position globally. And again, countries such as Singapore, Japan, and Korea, which have small public sectors, also make the top ten list. Clearly the Nordics are successful societies whose achievements are to be admired. But this success existed before the transition to high tax systems. Doesn't this tell us something?

TOP TEN COUNTRIES WITH LOWEST CHILD MORTALITY RATES

1960 (SMALL PUBLIC SECTORS IN NORDICS)	2000 (PEAK OF NORDIC WELFARE STATES)	2013 (LATEST DATA)
SWEDEN	SINGAPORE	ICELAND
NETHERLANDS	ICELAND	FINLAND
ICELAND	SWEDEN	JAPAN
NORWAY	FINLAND	NORWAY
AUSTRALIA	JAPAN	SINGAPORE
DENMARK	NORWAY	SWEDEN
SWITZERLAND	FRANCE	AUSTRIA
FINLAND	ITALY	DENMARK
UNITED KINGDOM	AUSTRIA	ITALY
FRANCE	DENMARK	KOREA

Under-five mortality rate is shown. Source: UN Inter-agency Group for Child Mortality Estimation (IGME) and own analysis. Modern comparable countries for which data exist have been compared. These are: Australia, Austria, Belgium, Canada, Denmark, Finland, France, Greece, Iceland, Ireland, Italy, Japan, Netherlands, Norway, Portugal, Czech Republic, Korea, Singapore, Spain, Sweden, Switzerland, UK, and USA. Some countries, such as Germany, have been excluded, since data from 1960 is not available. In 2000, Iceland and Singapore shared the first position with the same rate, while in 2015 Iceland was ahead of all other countries.

EQUALITY DUE TO LARGE WELFARE STATES?

Admirers of Nordic societies in particular point to the countries' even income distribution. Certainly, by distributing incomes and providing services such as universal health care, the welfare states do contribute to more equal incomes. Much like long life spans and low child mortality, however, even income distribution evolved in the Nordics before the transition to large welfare states. Historic data on income equality only exists for a small number of countries. Therefore, it is not possible to look at how the global top-ten list has evolved over time. Swedish economists Jesper Roine and Daniel Waldenström have, however, been able to compare historical rates of income inequality in Sweden, the United States, Canada, France, and the Netherlands. Their findings are quite astonishing. Already by 1920, well before the existence of a large-scale welfare state, Sweden had among the lowest levels of inequality within this group of countries. The two economists wrote, "We find that, starting from levels of inequality approximately equal to those in other Western countries at the time, the income share of the Swedish top decile drops sharply over the first eighty years of the twentieth century. Most of the decrease takes place before the expansion of the welfare state and by 1950 Swedish top income shares were already lower than in other countries."[11]

Much like long life spans and low child mortality, even income distribution evolved in the Nordics before the transition to large welfare states.

A recent paper by economists Anthony Barnes Atkinson and Jakob Egholt Søgaard similarly looks at the evolution of income equality in Denmark. The authors find that income equality evolved in Denmark during the last part of the nineteenth century and the first half of the twentieth century. Most of the shift toward higher equality happened before the introduction of a large public sector and high taxes. The same paper explains that equality in Sweden and Norway mainly grew until 1970; that is to say, during the period when the Nordic welfare states were still relatively modest in size. The shift toward equal incomes continued somewhat until the mid-1980s, and has since reversed to somewhat higher inequality. In short, for all three countries equality mainly evolved before large welfare states.[12]

My brother, Tino Sanandaji, wrote in another study: "American scholars who write about the success of the Scandinavian welfare states in the postwar period tend to be remarkably uninterested in Scandinavia's history prior to that period. Scandinavia was likely the most egalitarian part of Europe even before the modern era. For example, it was the only major part of Western Europe that never developed full-scale feudalism and never reduced its farmers to serfdom."[13]

Historic data for income equality only exists for a few countries, but modern data is easier to find. On the next page the present top-ten list of the most equal economies are shown. Certainly we can see that the Nordic countries all have equal wealth distributions. There is also another group of countries that share the top-ten list, namely Slovenia, the Slovak Republic, and the Czech Republic. Slovenia, in fact, has the highest income equality in the world. The common feature between these two groups of countries is not welfare policy or income distribution. Slovenia, the Slovak Republic, and the Czech Republic have lower, and relatively flat, taxes. What they do share with the Nordics is homogenous populations. A homogenous population means that the majority of citizens share the same culture. When this is the case, unsurprisingly, incomes are likely to be more similar than in countries with big differences in culture. In fact, we know that the large differences in culture in the United States is a main cause of high inequality.[14]

Why do American ideologues and politicians on the left want to copy Nordic policies rather than the policy of Slovenia, which has the highest income equality in the world? Is it because they prefer the policies of Denmark, where taxes amount to 51 percent of the economy (the highest rate in the world) over those in Slovenia, where taxes are 37 percent? Why not be inspired by the Czech Republic, with a 34 percent tax rate, or

TOP TEN COUNTRIES WITH LOWEST INCOME INEQUALITY 2010–2014 AVERAGE (LATEST DATA)

1.	Slovenia	6.	Czech Republic
2.	Denmark	7.	Finland
3.	Norway	8.	Belgium
4.	Iceland	9.	Sweden
5.	Slovak Republic	10.	Austria

Source: OECD Stat Extract

the Slovak Republic with a 31 percent tax rate?[15] Could it be that they prefer a high-tax system? Or is it because they don't understand that the common feature is the high level of homogeneity among populations whose cultures emphasize individual responsibility?

What, exactly, is responsible for this culture of success in Nordic societies? What—other than the common answer, social democracy—explains the admirable social outcomes they experienced even before introducing large welfare states? The next part of this book attempts to answer this question through a historical outlook and a comparison between Nordics on both sides of the Atlantic.

Part 2

THE NORDIC CULTURE OF SUCCESS

3

COFFEE-CONSUMING WORKAHOLICS

HAVE YOU EVER VISITED SWEDEN, Denmark, Norway, Finland, or Iceland? Perhaps even worked there? If so, I would wager that you have noticed that people who live there have a unique way of interacting with one another. For example, a strong sense of cooperation exists in most workplaces. Employers and employees pull in the same direction, and therefore management practices are often relaxed. Nordic companies can give employees a lot of freedom without sacrificing efficiency.[1] The book *Understanding Cross-Cultural Management* explains: "The Viking heritage of self-sufficiency, fairness, egalitarianism and democracy is reflected in the way Scandinavian business is run. In most companies, bosses are seen more as team leaders and groups facilitators as opposed to being decision makers who delegate tasks to others. As such, employees are often encouraged to express their opinions freely at meetings and everyone's opinion is given consideration when making decisions."[2]

People from the Nordics are valued as employees abroad, since the concept of strong Nordic work ethics is widely recognized.[3] When directly asked, the large majority of workers in the Nordics see themselves as totally committed to their employer. As the following comparison shows, this is not the case for most other countries in Europe.[4]

SHARE OF WORKERS IN EUROPE "TOTALLY COMMITTED TO THEIR EMPLOYER"

COUNTRY	PERCENT
POLAND	65
SWEDEN	65
NORWAY	63
DENMARK	53
NETHERLANDS	47
SWITZERLAND	46
LUXEMBOURG	45
IRELAND	44
BELGIUM	43
GERMANY	43
UNITED KINGDOM	42
FRANCE	41
ITALY	39
PORTUGAL	28
HUNGARY	25
RUSSIA	16

Source: Kelly Global Workforce Index (2010).

Perhaps you have noticed that your Swedish friend is always on time? And when you are five minutes late, she has a disappointed expression on her face. This is also a typical cultural trait. In *Cross-Cultural Business Behavior: A Guidebook for Those Who Work in Different Countries*, we read: "Business people from the four Nordic cultures definitely share a monochronic orientation to time. They value punctuality, follow meeting agendas and tend to adhere to schedules."[5] One of the first things I have taught my friends who have moved to Sweden is that they have to respect the clock. In other parts of the world, promising to show up for dinner at eight o'clock means that you will be there somewhere between eight or nine. In Sweden, it means that you should be ringing the doorbell exactly when a few minutes have passed after eight (since being early to dinner is a greater sin than being late). If it is a work meeting, you should instead be there a few minutes in advance. Another cultural feature that is connected to working life, and difficult to miss, is the Nordic obsession with coffee.

When David Kamp reviewed Stieg Larsson's hit Swedish crime trilogy for the *New York Times*, he expressed surprise about how many of the scenes revolved around servings of coffee: "Larsson's is a dark, nearly humorless world, where everyone works fervidly into the night and swills tons of coffee; hardly a page goes by without someone 'switching on the coffee machine,' ordering 'coffee and a sandwich' or responding affirmatively to the offer 'Coffee?'"[6] Roberto Ferdman replied in the *Atlantic* that "the coffee obsession has much less to do with Larsson than it does with Sweden." As Ferdman explains, the Nordic countries top the global rankings when it comes to the average number of coffee cups consumed. Finns, Swedes, Danes, and Norwegians gulp down more cups than Americans.[7] Indeed, as shown in the table below, coffee consumption is three times as high in Finland as in America.[8] Turkey and Italy, famous for their strong coffee, don't even come close. In these countries, small cups of thick coffee are consumed. In the United States, coffee is often served in large cups but is frequently quite weak. In the Nordics, the cups are both large and filled to the rim with strong coffee.

COFFEE CONSUMPTION PER PERSON IN SELECTED COUNTRIES

COUNTRY	CONSUMPTION PER DAY PER CAPITA
FINLAND	12.3 KG
NORWAY	9.7 KG
DENMARK	8.7 KG
SWEDEN	7.3 KG
ITALY	5.7 KG
UNITED STATES	4.2 KG
UNITED KINGDOM	2.8 KG
TURKEY	0.5 KG

Source. International Coffee Council (2012).

Researcher Taija Ojaniemi explains that the high rate of coffee consumption in his home country of Finland might seem as something of a puzzle. Coffee cannot be grown in Finland, or anywhere near it. Over the years, coffee consumption in the country has been restricted by legislation, economic crises, and periods of warfare. So why are Finns so addicted to the beverage? Ojaniemi theorizes that the culture of coffee drinking can be related to historic attempts to ban alcohol, as coffee can be seen as an alternate social drink. Another theory is that coffee consumption is related to working culture: "An average middle-aged Finn drinks most of his or her coffee during the statutory coffee breaks at work. These breaks are important social events that maintain the employees' working morale and group spirit. At many Finnish workplaces, the coffee is free and workers can drink as much as they like."[9]

[The Nordic preoccupation with coffee] is a vivid example of the long-term obsession Nordic societies have with creating a culture focused on hard work.

Coffee was introduced in the seventeenth century when Finland was still part of the Swedish Kingdom. The new drink was suspected of deteriorating the citizens' work ethics and the productive capacity of the nation. Ojaniemi explains: "Coffee was banned altogether four times in the eighteenth century on the grounds of its negative effect on the national economy, public health and work ethics."[10] The historical fear of coffee as a productivity inhibiter, and its modern embrace as a productivity enhancer, is a vivid example of the long-term obsession Nordic societies have had with creating a culture focused on hard work. But what is the origin of this unique mind-set? It seems that religion, climate, and history have all played a role in forming the Nordics into coffee-consuming workaholics.

Over a hundred years ago, German sociologist Max Weber observed that Protestant countries in northern Europe tended to have a higher living standard, better academic institutions, and overall more well-functioning societies than in other parts of Europe. He believed that the cause of the success of Protestant nations was to be found in a stronger "Protestant work ethic."[11] Swedish scholar Assar Lindbeck later built upon this theory by looking at factors other than religion. He explained that it has historically been difficult to survive as a farmer without working exceptionally hard in the hostile Scandinavian environment. The population, therefore, out of necessity adopted a culture with great emphasis on individual responsibility and hard work.[12] This is in line with the ideas put forth by Greek philosopher Aristotle, who already by the 300s BC observed that people in cold countries had to strive harder than those in warmer countries in order to survive.[13]

What is unique about Nordic countries is that they are not only cold, but have also through most of their recent history been dominated by independent farmers. In most other parts of the world, the majority of farmers did not own their land, and were instead landless workers, indebted laborers, or slaves. Groups such as Russian serfs could often face even greater hardship than the independent Nordic farmers. However, strong working ethics do not arise simply from hardship, but rather from a situation where hard work is clearly rewarded. The returns of intense labor and investments are much more significant in systems where property rights are extended to broad segments of the population. While Russian serfs got a meager reward even if they worked hard, Nordic farmers could enjoy the fruit of their labor. Nordic agriculture fared better than in Russia since the Nordics were early adopters of one of the key elements of the free market system: widespread property rights.[14] This corresponds with Thomas Jefferson's description of independent farmers in the United States as "the most virtuous and independent citizens."[15] The Nordic climate and economic system was thus for generations, well before the rise of industrialism, characterized by environmental and societal conditions that promoted norms related to work and responsibility.

A vivid example is given by a poem written by Swedish poet Johan Ludvig Runeberg. After a visit to the town of Saarijärvi in middle Finland during the 1820s, Runeberg wrote about the local population's harsh struggle for survival. The poem depicted the labors of the farmer Paavo, who strove to support his family by working the land in the inhospitable climate. Floods during the spring and hailstorms during the summer ruined much of the crops. The cold during the autumn destroyed the remainder. Paavo and his wife were forced to mix bark in their bread to survive the coming year, a common tradition among farmers in this part of the world. During the next year the Finnish farmer worked hard digging trenches to improve his farmland. Again however he was rewarded with a meager harvest due to unfortunate weather. The family mixed even more bark in their bread to survive the second year, and Paavo worked the land even harder. Finally, the third year's harvest was not destroyed by the weather. Paavo's wife happily exclaimed that they could now afford to eat regular bread. But Paavo insisted that they continue to mix in bark in their bread, since they ought to share food with their neighbors, whose harvest had been ruined by the cold.[16]

The United States will not simply transform to Sweden or

Denmark by expanding the size of government and raising taxes.

The descriptive poem illustrates that those who lived off the land in the harsh Nordic nations needed to have not only a stoic resolve to work hard and plan ahead, but also social trust and cohesion. Without hard work and cooperation, Paavo's family and their neighbors would find it difficult to survive. The poem also clearly illustrates that the independent farmers, in contrast to landless peasants in many other parts of the world, had much to gain from working to improve the productivity of their farms. These nuances of Nordic history don't seem to interest the admirers of Nordic-style social democracy in America. However, once we understand the deep-rooted cultural roots of Nordic achievement, we can better understand why the United States will not simply transform to Sweden or Denmark by expanding the size of government and raising taxes. It is the norms of cooperation, punctuality, honesty, and hard work that largely underpin Nordic success.

Historic sources show that Nordic people for generations have been seen as industrious and honest. An encyclopedia from 1834, for example, tells us, "The Swedes . . . bear the national character of bravery, frankness, honesty, and hospitality. . . . The men are in general tall, robust, sincere and industrious."[17] In another book, published the same year, Danish-French geographer and journalist Malte-Brun wrote about the excellent roads that had been built in Sweden, and how the civil rights of the peasantry were protected in Sweden as well as in Finland (which was part of Sweden at the time).[18] A history book about the Nordics, published in 1838, extends a similar description to the Norwegians: "The Norwegians may be considered an industrious people; but from the poverty and limited resources of the country, their genius is compelled to operate within a narrow sphere, and can rarely avail itself of extensive improvements."[19] The common theme from historic sources is that the Nordic people were honest and hardworking, doing their best to survive and thrive in their countries unforgiving climates. It is this historic heritage on which much of the region's current success rests. Perhaps we shouldn't be surprised that the same peoples in generations past, although their lands were rather unfruitful, conquered much of northern Europe, settled far-reached islands, and even established colonies in North America well before Christopher Columbus was born.

Although norms, values, and other aspects of social capital are inherently difficult to measure, they are nonetheless extremely important for creating well-functioning societies. A good illustration is how levels of trust vary between different societies. The more we trust strangers, the safer we feel. High levels of trust and trustworthiness also affect prosperity. The simple reason is that the more we can trust each other, the more we can trade and cooperate with others. From an anecdotal perspective, many individuals from Nordic countries who work abroad are told by their business associates that Nordic people are generally trustworthy. Researchers have shown that this view on trustworthiness has merit. In surveys the Nordic people indeed stand out as among the most trusting in the world.[20] A study by Jan Delhey and Kenneth Newton shows that the countries in the region combine all the features traditionally associated with high levels of trust. The authors wrote, "High trust countries are characterized by ethnic homogeneity, Protestant religious traditions, good government, wealth (gross domestic product per capita), and income equality. This combination is most marked in the high trust Nordic countries."[21]

High levels of trust, a strong work ethic, and social cohesion are the perfect starting point for successful economies. They are also the cornerstones of fruitful social democratic welfare policies. Of course, it is easier to introduce high taxes and generous welfare in countries that from the start have low poverty, few people willing to overuse welfare programs, many hardworking individuals, and a culture where people take care of their health.[22] A common notion is that politicians in the United States have opted to introduce less-generous public programs, perhaps since they care little for the need of the poor, while politicians in the Nordics have chosen a more progressive route. Several times during my travels in the United States, after hearing that I live in Sweden, Americans have told me something along this line: "In Sweden you have chosen a system where government takes much greater care of its citizens." But how much of this is because different arbitrary choices have been made in America? I would argue that much of the difference is because Americans live in a different culture than in the Nordics. Sure, different choices have been made, but they have been based on the different cultural circumstances.

We must account for the fact that welfare state policies have been more suited for Nordic societies than for the American. During the first half of the twentieth century, the Nordic countries had—as explained in chapter 2—similar-sized governments as the United States. Up to this point the policy direction in both regions was fairly similar. In fact, after the Great Depression American politicians such as Franklin D. Roosevelt were at least as enthusiastic about introducing wide-ranging welfare state programs as their counterparts in the Nordics. The common assumption that the United States early on chose a small government path while Scandinavia rapidly moved toward large welfare regimes is simply not true. In reality the American welfare system developed parallel to that of Scandinavian countries. But there was a major difference: American welfare met with early criticism, precisely because the unintended consequences of deteriorating norms and family breakup was so evident.

In homogenous Scandinavia this early criticism did not materialize, at least not on nearly the same scale. The uniquely strong norms associated with personal responsibility and work in the Nordics made these societies particularly well suited for avoiding the moral hazard of generous welfare systems. If America had the same levels of trust and work ethics, it would be more feasible to introduce Nordic-style social democracy. Without these attributes, the dreams of politicians such as Bernie Sanders will be difficult to achieve. Even if American politicians on the left were given free rein, I very much doubt that they would be able to transform the United States to a Nordic society. Sure, many ideologies believe this to be possible, but then again, ideologues have a tendency to vastly exaggerate the power of politics to change society.

Of course, one could argue that it's the other way around. Perhaps the Nordic countries have cooperation and high levels of trust because of the large welfare states. We shouldn't reject this notion out of hand. In theory it could be true. If people want to have a generous welfare system, and know that the system will only work if individuals are trustworthy and do not overuse welfare, then they might make a concerted effort to create a trustworthy society. So, do the Nordic countries have large welfare states since they began with high levels of trust, which allowed for generous welfare systems, or do they have widespread trust because this is the result of social democratic policies? In other words: did the chicken come first or the egg? By relying on the sophisticated methodology used by Swedish researcher Andreas Bergh and his Danish colleague Christian Bjørnskov, we can find the answer to this question.

A long tradition in psychology indicates that a basic sense of trust in strangers is instilled in individuals in early child-hood. This basic sense remains relatively stable for the rest of the individual's life, if not disturbed by major events. Indeed, high levels of trust seem to span over generations, as they are passed from parent to child. An important observation is that the trust levels of Americans closely follows the trust levels of the countries from which their ancestors came. And as it turns out, no group in the United States has as high trust levels as those with Scandinavian origins. Americans of Scandinavian decent even have slightly higher levels of trust than their cousins who inhabit the Scandinavian countries themselves.[23] This suggests that the origin of the Nordic culture of success predates modern welfare states. After all, large-scale migration of Nordic people to the United States occurred during the late nineteenth century and the early twentieth century, well before the shift toward large public sectors. Researchers Andreas Bergh and Christian Bjørnskov use a number of different statistical techniques to examine historic trust levels. They have concluded that historic trust levels are not caused by welfare state design, since welfare states are a relatively modern phenomenon. The authors explain: "Trust is high in universal welfare states, not because welfare state universality creates trust, but because trusting populations are more likely to create and sustain large, universal welfare states."[24]

[Only] trusting populations are more likely to create and sustain large, universal welfare states.

So it seems that the unique Nordic culture predates the welfare state. Additionally, this unique culture is found both in the citizens of Nordic nations as well as among Nordic Americans. How well, then, does the latter group, who combine the unique Nordic culture with living in the capitalist American society, fare? If we assume that Nordic-style social democracy is the key to success, we should expect this group to have poor results. If we believe that Nordic culture is what matters, we should expect Nordic Americans to be thriving. Comparing Nordic Americans with the Nordics is important in figuring out if it makes sense for America to adopt Nordic-style social democracy or not. The arguments made by admirers of democratic socialism in the United States are, after all, about comparing apples (Nordic people) with oranges (American people). When we compare apples (Nordic people) with apples (Nordic American people) we find that the core arguments of those such as Bernie Sanders simply vanish. If anything, the comparison of apples with apples is in favor of the American rather than the Nordic social system.

4

COMPARING APPLES TO APPLES

A KEY LESSON FROM THE success of the Nordics is that culture matters. We should not be surprised that it is these societies, with their strong ethics and sense of community, that managed to achieve even income distributions and good social outcomes before introducing large welfare states. Well before the public sector stepped in, churches and voluntary community groups were improving social conditions by emphasizing individual responsibility. The Nordic people were thought in their local communities to work hard, drink moderately, take care of their families, and help their neighbors. But of course, this success isn't limited to one side of the Atlantic. A large share of the Nordic population migrated to the United States during the nineteenth century. Although it was typically the less well-off families who sailed for prospects overseas, facing many difficulties and often starting new lives with empty hands, they prospered by relying on the same norms that had served them so well in their homelands.

Early Nordic immigrants to the United States, among others, began arriving during the seventeenth century to the small colony New Sweden around the Delaware Bay. Following the American Civil War, migrants from Scandinavia started to arrive in the United States in substantial numbers. Thanks to the Homestead Act of 1862—a government program that promised land ownership to pioneers who chose to settle undeveloped federal land west of the Mississippi—some of the most pronounced Nordic societies sprang up in the Midwest. Within a generation, Nordic migrant communities had spread from coast to coast. The migrants had to overcome many challenges in their new homeland, but seem to have been successfully assimilated. In the book *Immigrants in American History: Arrival, Adaptation, and Integration*, American historian Arnold Barton has written, "Compared with many other immigrant groups, the Swedes and other Scandinavians were on the whole well received by the older, dominant Anglo-American population in the new land. . . . They soon gained the reputation of being hardworking, honest, and reliable."[1] Similarly Eric Dregni explains in the book *Vikings in the Attic: In Search of Nordic America*, "The Swedish immigrants were very soon accepted as hard working and honest—if a bit dim due to their accents. In general, the Swedes quickly integrated and just as quickly dropped any reference to their previous life in Sweden. They fit in more quickly with mainstream American than any other ethnic group."[2]

Nordic migrants did face negative stereotypes and hostility, like many immigrant groups before them. However, their fellow Americans soon came to acknowledge the working ethics that the Nordics are famous for. Those who had traveled across the Atlantic did so to escape poverty. America offered them the chance for upward mobility. In 1910 George Erickson, a Swedish miner on the Gogebic Range, wrote in a letter home, "[I am] glad that I am not home but here where I am, for as far as the economy and working conditions are concerned America is far ahead of Sweden for a poor workingman. At the same time you have to be clever, a good worker, and reliable. A man who drinks a lot has no future here. There are so many people that they have demands on a man, but otherwise the Swedes are highly valued as workers, so highly that even if you go and ask for work the boss may ask if you are Swedish, in that case you get work right away."[3]

"The Swedish immigrants were very soon accepted as hard working and honest. . . They fit in more quickly with mainstream American than any other ethnic group." —ERIC DREGNI

The contributions of Nordic people to the United States are often forgotten. However, people from Nordic ancestry have played a key role in shaping American society. An example is Norman Borlaug, great-grandchild of Norwegian immigrants to the United States. Many Nordic Americans have won the Nobel Prize, but Borlaug was also awarded the Presidential Medal of Freedom and the Congressional Gold Medal for developing a high-yield, disease-resistant, semi-dwarf Mexican wheat during the 1940s. This may not seem all that exciting, but in fact Borlaug is credited with having launched the Green Revolution—wherein new technology and new strains made it possible to substantially increase global food output. For his achievements he has been called "the man who saved a billion lives."[4] Conrad Hilton, whose father was a Norwegian immigrant, founded Hilton Hotels, while John Hundale Lawrence, whose grandparents had come from Norway, pioneered the field of nuclear medicine. Danish immigrant Hans Christian Febiger was an American Revolutionary War commander, confidant of George Washington, and later treasurer of Pennsylvania.

There is no shortage of Swedish American engineers. Gideon Sundback made several key advances in the development of the zipper. Alexander Samuelson and his colleagues designed the famous original Coca-Cola bottle. Swedish American chemist Glenn Theodore Seaborg was the principal or codiscoverer of no fewer than ten elements. John Ericsson, a Swedish-American inventor, is regarded as one of the most influential mechanical engineers in history. He amongst others designed the US Navy's first screw-propelled steam-frigate, the USS *Princeton*, together with Captain Robert Stockton. A fatal accident happened during the speed trial of the frigate. Ericsson however redeemed himself by working together with industrialist Cornelius DeLamater in designing the USS *Monitor*. The ship, which was the first in the world with a rotating tower, played an important role in the American Civil War. Clarence Leonard Johnson's role in American defense is difficult to overstate, as he played an important part in the design of the various jet fighters that saw America through the Second World War and the Cold War. One of America's leading mathematicians, Lars Valerian Ahlfors, was of Finnish origin.

Nordic Americans are still thriving today. According to the U.S. Census, there are approximately eleven million Americans who either report to have origins in Sweden, Denmark, Norway, and Finland, or alternatively simply state that they have Scandinavian background (Icelandic Americans seem to be too few to measure).[5] Thus, if Nordic Americans formed their own nation, it would have a greater population than any one of the actual Nordic countries. It is worth comparing the social and economic outcomes of the eleven million Nordic Americans, with their nearly 25 million cousins in the actual Nordic countries.

As stated before in this book, Americans on average have a higher living standard than the population of the Nordics, with the exception of oil-rich Norwegians. Nordic Americans have, thanks to their uniquely successful culture, an even bigger advantage. As the following table shows, Danish Americans have fully 55 percent higher living standard than Danes.[6] Swedish Americans have similarly 53 percent higher standard than Swedes. The gap is even greater, 59 percent, between Finnish Americans and Finns. Even though Norwegian Americans lack the oil wealth of Norway, they have 3 percent higher living standard than their cousins overseas. These numbers are quite impressive. I would very much like to hear how proponents of Nordic-style social democracy would respond to them. Let's not forget: those people who migrated from the Nordics were the more impoverished ones, while the more affluent people often stayed behind.[7] If anything, the latter groups should be expected to be slightly ahead in living standard. However, the American economic system has evidently allowed people of Nordic origin to achieve a much higher living standard than the social democratic economic systems of the Nordics. When comparing apples with apples, we find that the choice between an American-style and a Nordic-style economic model seems to be a 50 percent higher living standard. High school graduation rates, another common metric of social advancement, is also in favor of Nordic Americans. At age twenty-five, around one in five in the Nordics has yet to graduate high school. As the following table shows, among Nordic Americans, fewer than one in twenty lacks a high school diploma at the same age.[8]

GDP PER CAPITA (US DOLLARS)[9]

DANISH AMERICANS	$70,925
SWEDISH AMERICANS	$68,897
SCANDINAVIAN AMERICANS	$68,081
NORWEGIAN AMERICANS	$67,385
NORWAY	$65,685
FINNISH AMERICANS	$64,774
ALL AMERICANS	$52,592
DENMARK	$45,697
SWEDEN	$45,067
FINLAND	$40,832

American Community Survey, OECD Stat Extract, and author's calculations. GDP per capita for Nordic American groups have been estimated by dividing their per capita incomes, as stated by the American Community Survey, with the average American per capita income. The number has thereafter been multiplied with the average GDP per capita in the United States. Based on 2013 data and 2013 rate of U.S. dollars.

HIGH SCHOOL GRADUATION RATES AMONG
THOSE 25 YEARS OR OLDER

COUNTRY	PERCENT
SCANDINAVIAN AMERICANS	97.3
SWEDISH AMERICANS	96.6
DANISH AMERICANS	96.5
FINNISH AMERICANS	96.4
NORWEGIAN AMERICANS	96.3
ALL AMERICANS	86.3
NORWAY	80.7
SWEDEN	79.6
FINLAND	78.0
DENMARK	75.1

American Community Survey, Eurostat database and author's calculations.
Based on 2013 data.

The tired, poor and huddled masses who migrated from the Nordic shores to the US have also over time largely escaped poverty.

So, it seems that the American system allows for higher prosperity and encourages more students to graduate high school. But what about social exclusion? To start, we can look at the unemployment rates of Nordic Americans and compare it to those living in the Nordic nations. Norway has a seemingly low unemployment rate, which, as you will see in a later chapter, is due to a system where true unemployment rates are hidden within welfare programs. Besides Norway, the Nordic countries have twice the unemployment rate of Nordic Americans, and also slightly higher rates than the average American.[10] The tired, poor and huddled masses who migrated from the Nordic shores have also over time largely escaped poverty. Nordic Americans have less than half the average American poverty rate. Danish Americans have as low as one-third of the national poverty rate (see the Poverty Rate table that follows).

UNEMPLOYMENT RATE[11]

COUNTRY	PERCENT
NORWAY	3.4
FINNISH AMERICANS	3.6
NORWEGIAN AMERICANS	3.7
SCANDINAVIAN AMERICANS	3.8
SWEDISH AMERICANS	3.9
DANISH AMERICANS	4.1
ALL AMERICANS	5.9
DENMARK	7.0
SWEDEN	8.1
FINLAND	8.2

American Community Survey, OECD Stat Extract. Calculations based on 2013 data. U.S. data for sixteen year and older. European data for fifteen and older.

Economists Geranda Notten and Chris de Neubourg have calculated the poverty rates in European countries and the United States using the same way of measuring poverty. They have shown that the absolute poverty rates in Denmark (6.7 percent) and Sweden (9.3 percent) are indeed lower than the American level (11 percent). For Finland, the rate (15 percent) is somewhat higher than in the United States.[12] But let's move from comparing apples with oranges to comparing apples to apples. The poverty rate of the Nordic Americans is, as the following table shows, between half and one-third of the average American level. Thus, the American capitalist system has allowed people from the Nordics to achieve lower poverty compared to the citizens of the Nordic countries. This is not an observation restricted to a single group. Scandinavian Americans, Swedish Americans, Finnish Americans, Norwegian Americans and Danish Americans all have lower poverty levels than in the Nordic countries themselves.[13]

POVERTY RATE WITHIN THE UNITED STATES (FAMILIES)

ETHNICITY	PERCENT
ALL AMERICANS	11.7
SCANDINAVIAN AMERICANS	5.1
SWEDISH AMERICANS	5.1
FINNISH AMERICANS	5.1
NORWEGIAN AMERICANS	4.7
DANISH AMERICANS	4.2

American Community Survey. Based on 2013 data.

So, what does this all tell us? To begin with, the comparison illustrates the point that culture matters. Many politicians, academics, and journalists believe that Nordic countries have admirable social outcomes simply because they have large welfare states. This book has previously shown that these countries reached these good outcomes before transitioning to large welfare states. In this chapter we can draw the conclusion that those of Nordic origin who live in the American system combine low poverty and low unemployment with high living standards. More specifically, Nordic Americans have around 50 percent higher living standard, half the unemployment rate, lower poverty, and higher high school graduation rates than their cousins in the Nordics. The case for adopting a Nordic social democratic model, as it is put forward by the Left in America, suddenly doesn't seem so convincing once we realize these facts. If anything, it is the American system that seems to shine brighter.

> Nordic Americans have around 50 percent higher living standard, half the unemployment rate, lower poverty, and higher high school graduation rates than their cousins in the Nordics.

I am not the first to make this observation. Many years ago, Nobel Prize–winning American economist Milton Friedman was talking to a Swedish economist, who told him, "In Scandinavia, we have no poverty." Friedman cleverly replied, "That's interesting, because in America, among Scandinavians, we have no poverty, either."[14] Although both economists somewhat overstated the case (there is some poverty in Scandinavia, and also limited poverty also among Scandinavian Americans), they both made accurate observations. And their observations tell us something: There may very well be good reasons to admire different aspects of Nordic policy, such as their income distribution or parental leave programs. But the main ingredient of Nordic success is without doubt culture rather than social democracy.

5

HOW CAN THE NORDICS TAX SO MUCH?

MANY VISITORS TO THE NORDICS ask the same question: how come people here are willing to pay such high taxes? This is not something that only nerds obsessed with politics, such as myself, ponder. Regular Americans, who otherwise have little appetite for discussing political economy, are often astonished by the fact that Danes and Swedes pay half of their hard-earned cash to the government. After all, Danes and Swedes are in most regards culturally similar to Americans, and few Americans would be willing to do the same. In part, the explanation is of course that the Nordic people get more government services and pay high taxes in return. But then again, politicians on the left in the United States have long proposed to combine more taxes with more generous welfare policies. So far, voters have largely rejected this trade-off. Why don't Americans accept Nordic-style taxes when offered Nordic-style welfare? The obsession that American politicians, journalists, and intellectuals on the left have with the Nordics is to a large degree about this question. The Left wants to transfer more money to the tax agency in the United States but finds little support for this. The best solution that they have come up with is to turn America into Denmark.

To begin with, we can observe that, yes, taxes are indeed higher in the Nordics. In fact, they are punishingly high for those with a good income. Danish researcher Henrik Jacobsen Kleven has elaborated on this issue in his research. He wrote, "The top marginal tax rates are about 60–70 percent in the Scandinavian countries as opposed to only 43 percent in the United States." This comparison, however, only captures part of the difference. Nordic countries also have generous public benefit programs, some of which are given to working families but withdrawn from those who have a high income. So, if you increase your income, you pay more taxes and get less public transfers. Therefore, a Nordic person increasing her or his income by a hundred kronor could in certain situations gain only around twenty kronor, with the remaining eighty kronor going to the pockets of the government. By contrast, Kleven calculates that in the United States around sixty-three dollars are typically left in the pocket of the high-income worker, while thirty-seven dollars go to the government.[1]

If we introduced Nordic-style social democracy, does it suddenly become possible to heavily tax people without reducing prosperity?

Some people believe that the Nordic experience proves that punishingly high taxes are a viable policy. Is it true that Denmark and Sweden have stumbled upon a magical economic system wherein taxes simply stop mattering? If we introduced Nordic-style social democracy, does it suddenly become possible to heavily tax people without reducing prosperity? The answer is, of course, no. Remember how in the last chapter we found that Nordic Americans have a level of prosperity that is about 50 percent higher than that of their cousins in the Nordic countries? The best explanation for this significant gap is the higher Nordic tax rates. In most other areas of economic policy, the Nordic countries are as competitive as the United States. For example, they are open to trade, investments, and entrepreneurship. The main thing holding them back is the tax burden, which punishes hard work, education, and business ownership.

American economist Arthur Laffer is famous for explaining that when taxes are increased by a dollar, this doesn't mean that the government will gain an additional dollar. The reason is that taxes affect our decisions. When people face higher rates, they work fewer hours and less intensely. Young people choose not to study, or to study easier subjects to earn degrees. Firms invest less and competition is reduced. Taxes in effect shrink the economic output. So, when they are increased by a dollar, perhaps revenues will only increase by eighty cents. Or, if taxes are increased from an already high to an even higher level, the effect of raising them might be so severe that revenues only increase by fifty cents. At some theoretical point, taxes will be so high that if they are raised, the revenues will not increase at all.

That taxes affect our decisions is widely known. However, the idea that there is a tipping point at which increasing them actually leads to no change in revenues, or even to reduced revenues, is often taken as a theoretical notion. When would taxes in reality become so damagingly high? A study by the European Central Bank found that this tipping point is not just some whacky theory. Sweden already seems to have reached it. According to the study, the average tax on labor in the country is at the point where raising it would lead to very little if any increase in revenues. On the other hand, reducing taxes a little would lead to the same, or almost the same, amount being collected by the government. Tax rates in Denmark and Finland are also shown to be close to this extreme case. For taxation of capital, both Denmark and Sweden are shown to be on an even more extreme point: where more taxes lead to fewer revenues.[2]

Several other studies point in the same direction.[3] For instance, economist Åsa Hansson has calculated the efficiency loss for each additional Swedish krona levied and spent by the government. She explains that if the government collects an additional krona from a person who is already paying a high tax rate, the economy is negatively affected since work and entrepreneurship are punished. If the additional money collected by the government is spent on transfer programs that are an alternative to work, the economy is again damaged since people are encouraged to rely on the public rather than their own work incomes. Taken together, these effects are calculated to shrink the Swedish economy by three kronor for each krona collected and distributed by the government.[4]

To understand how taxes can have such a negative effect on the economy, consider a Swedish earner who is paying the maximum marginal tax rate and consuming her or his earnings. A payroll tax of 32 percent is paid on top of the gross wage.

Then, an average municipal tax of 32 percent and a state tax of 25 percent are collected. Finally, an average tax of 21 percent is added on top of the value of goods and services consumed. A government report has calculated that the total effective marginal tax rate, including all these taxes, amounts to 73 percent.[5] The report, published by the Swedish government, admits that the rate is so high that lowering it is expected to lead to more rather than less revenues.[6] So, the next time your friend doubts that tax cuts sometimes can in fact increase revenues, remind her or him that Swedish economists writing on behalf of the government say it is so.

In a report for the Confederation of Swedish Enterprise, professor Lennart Flood and economist Peter Ericsson similarly conclude that the high marginal taxes in Sweden reduce the number of available jobs substantially while being so damaging that they have little if any success in raising government revenues.[7] Danish studies point in the same direction.[8] The transition toward punishingly high rates has been anything but smooth. Danish think tank CEPOS (Center for Politiske Studier) calculates that increased taxes have over time crowded out direct household spending. Therefore, the private spending of the average Danish citizen dropped from being the sixth highest in the world in 1970 to being the fourteenth highest in 2011. According to CEPOS' report, Sweden experienced a fall from eighth to sixteenth position during the same period.[9] So, if anything, the lesson from the Nordics is that taxes truly can be quite damaging if allowed to reach high levels. But this only makes the question of why the people in the region are willing to pay such high rates even more puzzling.

If we return to the study by Danish researcher Henrik

Jacobsen Kleven, we find an interesting answer: "Scandinavia features higher levels of trust than anywhere else in the world. This evidence is consistent with the notion that social cohesion is larger in Scandinavian countries, which may explain their willingness to pay large taxes."[10] The unusually high levels of trust in the Nordics—which, as we have previously seen, have historical roots and exist among Nordic Americans as well as the Nordics themselves—make it possible to levy high taxes. Philipp Doerrenberg and his coauthors gave a similar explanation in a paper titled "Nice Guys Finish Last: Do Honest Taxpayers Face Higher Tax Rates?" In this case, the title tells it all. The researchers found that governments exploit groups with high relative levels of tax morale by taxing them more.[11] So, yes, it makes sense to say that Nordic people are willing to pay more taxes since they receive more from the government than Americans do. But there is also another explanation: again, culture. In societies that lack Nordic tax morale, it will likely be quite difficult to have tax rates as high as in Denmark and Sweden. It is certainly possible in theory to introduce Danish tax levels in the United States. But should we really expect the public to pay these rates?

There is also another explanation that is worth keeping in mind: taxes are hidden from the general public in the Nordics. You can try this for yourself. Ask a Swede why people with normal wages in the country are paying around half of their income to the tax agency. You might be rewarded with a puzzled face. Most Swedes think that normal earners are merely paying around a third of their income in taxes. The true rates have cleverly been hidden from sight. A historical perspective can help us understand the development of hidden taxes in the

Nordics. Before policies steered to the left in the late 1960s, the tax levels in the region were around 30 percent of GDP—quite typical of other developed nations at the time. Up to this point in time, most taxation occurred through direct taxes, which showed up on employees' pay stubs. However, politics started changing. Over time, an increasing share of taxation was to be raised through indirect taxes.

The most important form of indirect taxation is the employer's fee. This is a tax on labor, which has a very similar effect as the income tax. The difference is that it is called a fee rather than a tax, and that its name suggests that the employer rather than the employee is paying it. In effect, when somebody receives a wage of 10,000 kronor in Sweden, the employer has to pay additionally around 10,000 kronor to the government. Half of this is the tax on labor, and the other half is the employer's fee. On their pay stubs people see that their official wage is around 15,000 kronor, out of which 5,000 have been paid in taxes. The other 5,000 kronor, which has been paid to the tax authority, is often not even included on the pay stub. Of course researchers and government records acknowledge that the employer's fee is an indirect tax on labor, but people who don't know the fine print of the tax system are largely unaware of the fact that both direct and indirect taxes on labor exist. Thus, many ordinary citizens think the tax on labor is around a third of the income (5,000 kronor out of 15,000) rather than the actual rate of around half the income (10,000 kronor out of 20,000). Another form of an indirect tax is the value-added tax (VAT). In the United States, a sales tax is added to sold goods and services. Nordic countries used to have the same system. Over time they have moved toward a VAT, wherein the tax is hidden in the final price of the goods or service.

The four graphs that follow show the evolution of taxes in the Nordic countries over time. They all paint a similar picture: politicians in the Nordic countries did not introduce large welfare states by raising the direct taxes. Instead they hiked revenues by expanding indirect taxes. Interestingly, all of this had been predicted a long time before it actually happened. In 1903 Italian economist Amilcare Puviani explained that politicians would have incentives to hide the cost of government by levying indirect rather than direct taxes. By doing so, the public would be fooled into underestimating the true cost of having a large public sector.[12] Nobel Prize winner James Buchanan has expanded on the idea that it is easier for politicians to raise taxes that are hidden rather than visible ones.[13] Another Nobel Prize winner who has raised the same issue is Swedish economist Bertil Ohlin. In 1973 he wrote an article in a leading Swedish daily paper, explaining how the government at the time was systematically hiding the true tax level. Ohlin described how the Social Democrats in Sweden had realized that the general public were not keen on embracing higher taxes, and had thus chosen to hide the true rate.[14]

On average Swedes believed that taxes on work and consumption amounted to 40 percent of the wage of an average worker. The true level at the time was 60 percent.

HIDDEN AND VISIBLE TAXES IN FINLAND

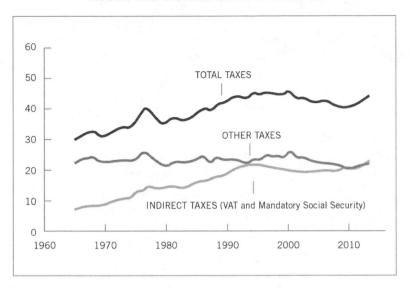

HIDDEN AND VISIBLE TAXES IN DENMARK

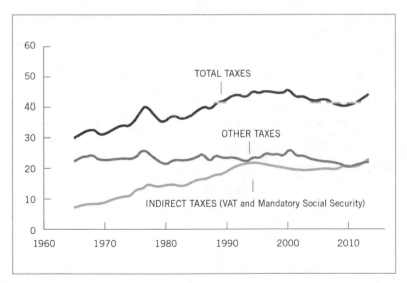

HIDDEN AND VISIBLE TAXES IN NORWAY

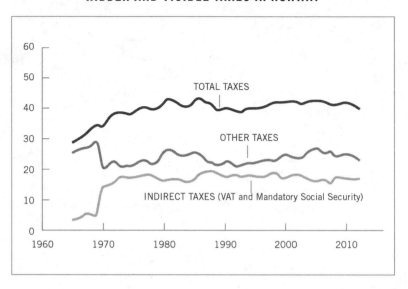

HIDDEN AND VISIBLE TAXES IN SWEDEN

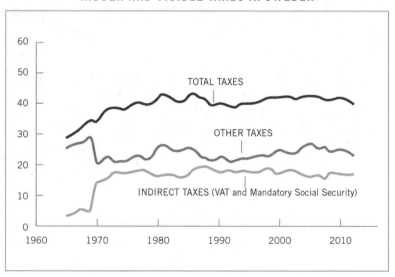

In a survey conducted in 2003, the Swedish public was asked to estimate the total amount of taxes they paid. Respondents were reminded to include all forms of direct and indirect taxation. On average Swedes believed that taxes on work and consumption amounted to 40 percent of the wage of an average worker. The true level at the time was 60 percent.[15] In 2015 the survey was repeated. Now the tax level had been reduced to 52 percent. The average respondent believed it to be 34 percent.[16] So, both surveys found that a third of the actual tax burden was hidden from the general public. This all shines a new light on Nordic-style social democracy. It is only a half-truth that the people in this part of the world are willing to put up with high taxes in return for generous welfare. If politicians hadn't hidden the tax bill, it would have proven quite difficult to raise the level. It remains to be seen if American politicians manage to copy this Nordic strategy of hiding the true burden of government or not. Taxes in America are, for all their flaws, still quite visible. Will they remain so for long?

Part 3

THE FAILURE OF NORDIC SOCIALISM

6

NORDIC FREE-MARKET SUCCESS
AND THE FAILURE OF THIRD-WAY
SOCIALISM

A FEW YEARS AGO, U.S. National Public Radio ran a story "about a country that seems to violate the laws of the economic universe." The country has "one of the lowest poverty rates in the world, low unemployment, a steadily growing economy and almost no corruption" although it has high taxes. That country is Denmark.[1] A popular myth among American liberals is that the Nordic countries somehow manage to defy standard economic logic by prospering despite large welfare systems and state involvement in the economy. Social democrats in the Nordics are also fond of this myth. Sweden's former social democratic prime minister Göran Persson has compared the country's economy to a bumblebee: "With its overly heavy body and little wings, supposedly it should not be able to fly—but it does."[2] In reality, however, there is nothing mysterious about Nordic prosperity. These countries grew rich when they combined free-market policies with low taxes and limited state involvement in the economy. A turn toward socialism crippled growth, while a new wave of market reforms again opened up for increased prosperity. In fact, it is difficult to find a region on Earth whose history shows us as clearly as the Nordics the importance of sound economic policies.

In 1943 Irish historian James Beddy asked a simple question: how come Denmark had grown so much more prosperous than Ireland? Based on a thorough statistical analysis, he concluded that Denmark had a national income per head that was almost 50 percent higher than in Ireland. But natural factors, such as average temperature, hours of sunshine, rainfall, and abundance of mineral resources all favored Ireland. Seven decades ago, the success of Denmark was already something of a puzzle. And the answer was not the welfare state, since the Danish welfare state was just beginning to take form during the 1940s. Social democratic policies came after Denmark grew rich. Beddy wrote:

> Denmark is not only a smaller country than Eire but her climate is less equable, her soils are, in general, lighter and poorer, she has no coal and no water power to compensate for its absence, nor has she any iron ore or other metallic ores to serve as a basis for industrial activities. Yet, in comparison with Eire, she has a bigger population, a greater agricultural output, a more extensive industrial system, a larger foreign trade, a lower national debt, a higher national income and a better standard of living.[3]

According to the Irish economist, the main reason for Denmark's success was that its economic system differed from that of Ireland. Ireland could learn from Denmark by focusing on "stimulating maximum profitable agricultural activity" and taking greater advantage of international trade. A key element was that the new "system shall be free from the restrictive effects of [Ireland's] present one."[4] In other words, Denmark was richer than Ireland despite a less favorable climate and fewer natural resources, since it relied more on market forces. Half a century later, Kevin O'Rourke expanded on this analysis. The Irish professor of economic history explored the structural and social differences that had existed between Ireland and Denmark in the late nineteenth century. According to O'Rourke, the latter country's greater prosperity has several explanations. Denmark had a homogenous culture coupled with political stability. Ireland was, on the other hand, culturally and politically divided. Danish society benefited from higher levels of trust and social capital. This can explain why cooperative businesses, such as creameries, could more easily be founded and run by milk farmers in Denmark than in Ireland. The countries also had different backgrounds when it came to how policies had developed. Denmark was an independent nation, the market-friendly policies of which had resulted from Danish decisions. Irish economic freedom was a product of British imperialism. Reforms transferring land ownership from the feudal class to the broader public had occurred much earlier in Denmark than in Ireland. O'Rourke explained that Irish farmers had limited access to the capital they needed to grow. On the other hand, small local savings banks in Denmark supplied credit even to those with little or no security for loans.[5]

In another publication, O'Rourke explains how the lack of market forces resulted in Ireland being slower in adapting novel technologies for dairy production than Denmark—an important business at the time for both nations. The Danish culture, with stronger social and political cohesion, also played an important role in this regard:

> Separators and cooperatives spread much more quickly in Denmark than in Ireland, despite the fact that both countries were important dairy producers, located in north-west Europe, and selling to the same market . . . property rights and social capital played a crucial role in determining the extent to which these two innovations were adopted: a lack of social and political cohesion, uncertain property rights as well as cultural factors all help explain why Ireland lagged behind Denmark during this period.[6]

So, in other words, already, before social democratic policies were introduced, Denmark was surprisingly prosperous. It certainly wasn't socialism that made Denmark rich, but rather, capitalism coupled with a culture of high trust, social cohesion, and a spirit of cooperation. Other research has shown that already during the latter half of the nineteenth century, well before the introduction of social democratic policies, Denmark was thriving, thanks to entrepreneurship.[7] Denmark's closest neighbor to the north was more of a late bloomer. However, few other nations have demonstrated as clearly as Sweden the phenomenal economic growth that comes from adopting free-market policies. Sweden was a poor nation before the 1870s, which explains the massive immigration to the United States that was taking place at the time. As a capitalist system evolved out of the agrarian society, the country grew richer. Property rights, free markets, and the rule of law combined with large numbers of well-educated engineers and entrepreneurs. These factors created an environment in which Sweden enjoyed an unprecedented period of sustained and rapid economic development.

It is often believed that the ideas of economic liberty were first expressed by Adam Smith... In fact, Anders Chydenius, a Finnish priest and a member of Sweden's Parliament, beat him to it.

It is often believed that the ideas of economic liberty were first expressed by Adam Smith, the father of modern economics, who in 1776 wrote his magnum opus, *An Inquiry into the Nature and Causes of the Wealth of Nations*. In fact, Anders Chydenius, a Finnish priest and a member of Sweden's Parliament, beat him to it. In 1765 Chydenius published the pamphlet *Den Nationnale Winsten*, which translates to *The National Gain*. There he explored the relationship between economy and society, argued that free trade and free industry created prosperity, and laid out the principles of capitalism as well as modern democracy. It would take around a century until Sweden embraced Chydenius's ideas. Johan August Gripenstedt, who in the late nineteenth century served as finance minister, was responsible for opening up the country for free trade, building a modern railway infrastructure and reducing government involvement in the economy. Without doubt, Sweden's path toward prosperity was cleared by these reforms.

In the hundred years following the shift toward capitalism, Sweden experienced phenomenal economic development. Famous Swedish companies such as IKEA, Volvo, Tetra Pak, H&M, Ericsson, and Alfa Laval were all founded during this period, and were aided by business-friendly economic policies and low taxes.[8] It is sometimes claimed that Sweden's high growth rate is a result of social democratic policies. In fact, much of the development occurred between the time when free markets were introduced (circa 1870) and the start of the era dominated by Social Democrat rule (circa 1936). As shown in the following table, during this period Sweden had the fastest growth rate among European nations. The other Nordic countries followed closely after. In part, this might be explained by the region

GROWTH DURING FREE MARKET ERA (1870 TO 1936)[9]

COUNTRY	PERCENT GROWTH
SWEDEN	2.0
NORWAY	1.7
FINLAND	1.6
SWITZERLAND	1.6
DENMARK	1.6
GERMANY	1.3
FRANCE	1.2
ITALY	1.1
UNITED KINGDOM	1.0
NETHERLANDS	1.0
BELGIUM	0.9
AUSTRIA	0.7

catching up to the rest of Europe. There is, however, no doubt that the Nordics benefited from their market-friendly policies.

When Nordic social democrats came to power, they were initially quite pragmatic. Rather than killing the capitalist goose that had been laying all the golden eggs, they nurtured it while slowly introducing welfare programs. This all changed during the late 1960s and early 1970s, when social democrats in Sweden, and to a less extent also in the other Nordic countries, radicalized and moved toward socialism. The region thus had an early social democrat era, where much of the free-market policies were kept in place, and a later social democrat era when the true shift toward socialism occurred. As shown in the following table, the Nordic nations fell behind the rest of Europe

GROWTH DURING EARLY SOCIAL DEMOCRAT ERA (MODERATELY FREE MARKETS) 1936–1970[10]

COUNTRY	PERCENT GROWTH
AUSTRIA	3.5
ITALY	3.4
FINLAND	3.2
SWITZERLAND	3.1
FRANCE	3.0
SWEDEN	2.9
NORWAY	2.7
GERMANY	2.7
NETHERLANDS	2.5
DENMARK	2.4
BELGIUM	2.3
UNITED KINGDOM	1.7

during the early social democratic era, but retained a moderate level of development.

Fans of Nordic-style democratic socialism admire the policies that were introduced in the Nordics, and particularly so in Sweden, around 1970 and onward. The only problem is that this shift in economic policy was a major failure. The *Economist* explains: "In the period from 1870 to 1970 the Nordic countries were among the world's fastest-growing countries, thanks to a series of pro-business reforms such as the establishment of banks and the privatization of forests. But in the 1970s and 1980s the undisciplined growth of government caused the reforms to run into the sands."[11] Around 1968 the Left radicalized around the world, fueled by the criticism of the Vietnam War. The social democrats in Sweden and other Nordic countries grew bold, and decided to go after the goose that lay the golden eggs: entrepreneurship. It was finally time to stop being pragmatic and really start challenging the capitalist system. Time to put democratic socialism to the test.

One way of achieving this was to tax the rich, and business owners, as much as possible. Economist Magnus Henrekson has shown that taxes in Sweden rose to such an extent that successful business owners could actually lose money by making a profit. This absurd situation existed because high marginal taxes coupled with high inflation. If a Swedish business invested a million kronor to create a profit, one year later the business might have less money left after it had paid hefty taxes on the profits, while high inflation had reduced the value of the original sum invested. Henrekson concluded that the tax policies "developed according to the vision of a market economy without individual capitalists and entrepreneurs."[12] Not surprisingly, the sharp left turn in economic policy markedly affected entrepreneurship. Sten Axelsson, another Swedish economist, has shown that the period between the end of the nineteenth century and the beginning of the First World War was a golden age for the founding of successful entrepreneurial firms. After 1970, however, the establishment of new firms dropped significantly. Sweden became strongly dependent on firms that had been formed generations ago.[13]

How can the dramatic fall in entrepreneurship be explained? One reason might be that it takes time for firms to grow large. Another is that large firms played a more vital part in the economy in previous times. However, these factors alone cannot explain the massive reduction in the number of new entrepreneurial firms in Sweden. Clearly, one important factor is the changes in economic policy, toward the famous Third Way between socialism and free markets. These policies culminated in the introduction of employee funds at the beginning of the 1980s. The idea was to confiscate parts of companies' profits and use them to buy shares of the same companies. The shares would in turn be part of funds controlled by labor unions. In effect, the system was designed to gradually transform the ownership of private companies to the unions a soft evolution toward socialism. Although the system was abolished before it could turn Sweden into a socialist economy, it did manage to drive the founders of IKEA, Tetra Pak, H&M, and other highly successful firms away from the country.

> Third Way socialist policies are . . . a failed social experiment, which resulted in stagnating growth and which with time have been abandoned.

Third Way socialist policies are often upheld as the normal state of Swedish policies. In reality, one can better understand them as a failed social experiment, which resulted in stagnating growth and which with time have been abandoned.[14]

Interestingly, even the leading Social Democrats at the time seem to have been aware of the damage that Third Way policies were doing. The most striking example relates to the introduction of the employee funds. Kjell-Olof Feldt, one of Sweden's leading Social Democrats through history and at the time the finance minister, had to debate the benefits of the funds in the Swedish Parliament. But the minister was uneasy. During the debate, he was scribbling on a piece of paper. A reporter took a photograph of a poem that the minister wrote down. Remarkably, it turned out that the finance minister was anything but enthusiastic about the funds. In fact, he believed them to be very damaging for the country. Feldt went as far as describing the employee funds with profanity. A loose translation of the poem is:

> The employee funds are a [profanity],
>
> but now we have dragged them all this way.
>
> Then they will be filled with every bigwig,

that has supported us in our struggle.

Now we don't have to go any more rounds,

until the whole of Sweden is full of funds.

Kjell-Olof Feldt had good reasons to be critical of the radical ideas championed and introduced by his own party. In October 1983, a few months before Feldt scribbled profanity to describe the socialist policies, what is likely to have been the largest political demonstration in Swedish history was arranged. Upwards of one hundred thousand people marched against the employee funds. Although the social democratic leadership seems to have been aware that the funds were a bad idea, they had invested too much political prestige in the idea to back away from it. The funds were introduced in 1984, and later abolished following the election of a center-right government in 1991. The confiscation of profits for the funds were stopped by the new government and the money previously gathered in the funds was transferred into pension savings and research foundations. Sweden chose to return to the path of market economics over that of socialism. Foreign admirers of social democracy might be surprised by this fact, but the period between 1970 and 1991, when democratic socialism was put to the test, was a colossal failure for Sweden. As shown in the following table, Sweden had poor growth when compared to other parts of Europe. Denmark never embraced socialism as strongly as Sweden, but did swell up the welfare state. Again, the result was stagnation. Norway, on the other hand, prospered, thanks to having, literally, struck oil.

Since then, Nordic nations have implemented major market liberalizations to compensate for the growth-inhibiting effects

GROWTH DURING THIRD WAY SOCIALIST ERA 1970–1991[15]

COUNTRY	PERCENT GROWTH
NORWAY	3.1
AUSTRIA	2.8
ITALY	2.6
BELGIUM	2.4
FINLAND	2.4
FRANCE	2.1
GERMANY	2.1
UNITED KINGDOM	2.0
DENMARK	1.9
NETHERLANDS	1.8
SWEDEN	1.4
SWITZERLAND	1.1

of taxes, large welfare states, and labor market regulations. Denmark has even moved toward a flexible labor market. Clearly, the Nordic countries have learned their lessons from the failures of socialism. Today few, even among the hard left, openly point to the Swedish Third Way policies as a positive experience. The return to free markets has served the Nordics well. As shown on the following table,[16] the countries are again prospering. Denmark, which has, contrary to Sweden, not reduced its very high taxes, is the only one lagging behind.

But what about jobs? The transition toward socialism didn't only reduce growth and entrepreneurship in Sweden. The same policies also led to a significant crowding out of private job growth. Between 1950 and 2000, the Swedish population grew

GROWTH DURING THE NEW MARKET-REFORM ERA 1991–2014

COUNTRY	PERCENT GROWTH
UNITED KINGDOM	1.8
SWEDEN	1.8
NORWAY	1.8
FINLAND	1.8
NETHERLANDS	1.6
AUSTRIA	1.5
BELGIUM	1.4
GERMANY	1.3
DENMARK	1.2
FRANCE	1.1
SWITZERLAND	1.0
ITALY	0.3

Source: OECD Stat Extract.

from seven to almost nine million. The net job creation in the private sector was astonishingly enough close to zero during the same period (see graph). This teaches us a valuable lesson: if the government is expanded rapidly, private-sector job creation can indeed come to a halt. Perhaps admirers of democratic socialism would argue that this is no problem, since the public sector can grow with new jobs. During the period that private-sector job growth came to a halt, Swedish Social Democrats were fond of arguing that it was the government's responsibility to create new employment. Let's look at the development in the country to see how this plan turned out.

Jobs in the public sector did expand significantly until the end of the 1970s. After this point it became difficult to further increase the size of the already large public sector—simply because taxes had already reached such a high level that it was not plausible to raise them further. When the welfare state could grow no larger, the job market came to a complete halt, as neither the private sector nor the public one could grow larger. The stagnation ended after wide-ranging market reforms, including a lowering of the highest marginal taxes, were introduced in the early 1990s. In recent years, Sweden has become synonymous with strong job growth. But this is after a second wave of market reforms, and significant tax cuts, were introduced after a center-right government came to power in 2006.[17] Again, American observers can learn much from Sweden. A lesson is that democratic socialism and an aggressive expansion of the size of government can stop job growth. Another is that market reforms and tax reductions can spur job creation.

Democratic socialism . . . can stop job growth [while] market

reforms and tax reductions can spur job creation.

The stagnation of job growth that followed the rise of the Swedish welfare state slowly but surely changed the political landscape in Sweden. Particularly since the beginning of the 1990s, the policy debate has been focused on tackling exclusion from the job market. The reason is that around one million Swedes of working age have become trapped in visible and hidden unemployment. This might not seem like much to an

PUBLIC-SECTOR AND PRIVATE-SECTOR JOBS GROWTH IN SWEDEN (THOUSANDS)[18]

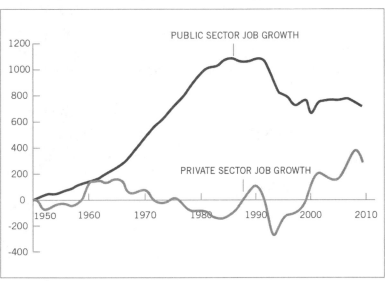

international audience, but keep in mind that Sweden has a population of fewer than ten million. Although market reforms and tax reductions have had some success in promoting job growth, the labor market exclusion persists. The situation is quite similar in the other Nordic nations.

To truly understand how social democratic policies affect the labor market, we can look at two different economic crises. One crisis occurred during the period when Sweden had low taxes and free markets. The other struck when the nation instead had high taxes and a large public sector. The first crisis was the Great Depression. As a trade-dependent nation, Sweden was not only hurt by the global economic depression, but also by the trade barriers other nations put up in a misguided effort to protect their economies from the downturn. From 1930 to 1933 the number of job opportunities available in Sweden decreased by 170,000—one-sixteenth of all jobs in the economy were lost. The crisis could have been severe, especially since it occurred at the same time that many young Swedes were entering the labor force. But the Great Depression was short-lived in Sweden. Job creation soon outpaced job destruction in the dynamic economy. As shown on the following graph, more Swedes were working in 1935 than before the crisis.[19]

EMPLOYMENT IN SWEDEN (THOUSANDS) BEFORE AND AFTER THE GREAT DEPRESSION

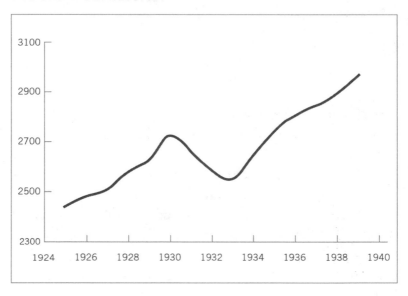

Source: Olle Krantz (1997)

The strong recovery was made possible by new, innovative businesses. During the crisis years, Nohab Flight engines (today known as Volvo Aero), was born. Shortly after the crisis, Securitas and SAAB were founded. A new method for creating paper pulp was invented, leading to the creation of Sunds Defibrator (today Metso Paper, a leading developer of paper industry equipment).[20] To this date, Sweden continues to rely heavily on businesses started during or shortly after the Great Depression. Opportunities were created across the Nordics during the crises. The ability to turn around the crises illustrates the benefits of combining the Nordic culture of success with free-market policies. As Norwegian economist Ola Honningdal Grytten puts it, "During the years of depression, entrepreneurs had to come up with new innovations in order to survive. New technology was utilized in the manufacturing industry. Production became more efficient and was better matched with the actual demand. Nordic manufacturing industry was by this able to operate at larger markets. In addition, cost efficient production gave competitive advantage to Nordic companies. Thus, exports increased." Grytten explains that the four Nordic nations indeed faced a significant decrease in economic production and a corresponding increase in unemployment during the Great Depression. "However, the crisis was milder and shorter than in most other Western economies at the time."[21]

So, let's compare the Great Depression with another downturn. The beginning of the 1990s saw a banking crisis hit the Swedish economy. In a time when unemployment was falling in many other countries, it rose rapidly in Sweden. Even when the country returned to economic growth, employment only slowly recovered. In fact, as shown in following graph, it took until 2008 before it had reached the pre-1990 level—ironically, the same year that a major global crisis hit the world.[22] A study from McKinsey has analyzed the paradox of why such a sluggish job development could occur in a time when the country was experiencing strong growth. The study concludes that labor market regulation and high taxes—staples of social democratic policies—explain the stagnation: "Labor market barriers are the main reason for the private service sector's failure to create new jobs. High taxes on employment raise the cost of labor for all employers and make low value-added services—undertaken, for instance, by restaurants, retailers, cleaning firms, and builders—very expensive."[23]

EMPLOYMENT IN SWEDEN (THOUSANDS) BEFORE AND AFTER THE 1990S CRISIS

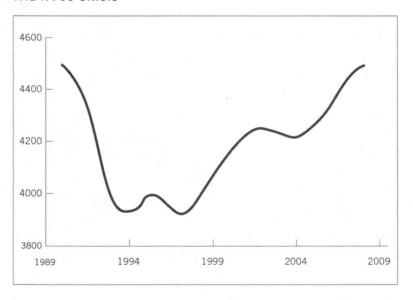

Source: Statistics Sweden (2009).

Finland also went through an economic crisis during the beginning of the 1990s. According to researchers Seppo Honkapohja and Erkki Koskela, the crisis can be understood as "a story of bad luck and bad policies." The bad luck was due to the collapse of the Soviet Union, an important trade partner for Finland. The bad policies included a tax system that was unfriendly to entrepreneurs and stringent financial regulations. In response to the crisis, taxes rose. Together with high levels of debt among Finnish firms and exchange rate depreciation, this slowed down the recovery. The authors concluded, "In the absence of bad policies, Finland would have experienced a recession, not a depression."[24] Summing up the experience from the respective crises faced by Finland and Sweden during the 1990s, Klas Fregert and Jaakko Pehkonen wrote that institutional factors, such as growth-inhibiting taxes, explain why the recovery from the crises was sluggish for both nations. During the following years, reforms were introduced in both countries, which helped recovery. These included reduced generosity in unemployment benefits, tax reforms, and less union dominance over the labor market. The reforms resulted in a substantial decrease in unemployment.[25]

Nordic countries have grown rich during periods with free-market policies and low taxes, and they have stagnated under socialist policies

It is still a common belief in countries such as the United States that Nordic countries somehow defy normal economic laws by prospering and creating jobs despite high taxes and large welfare states. But is there really any support for this theory? As we have seen, Nordic countries have grown rich during periods with free-market policies and low taxes, and they have stagnated under socialist policies. Job growth follows the same logic. Perhaps proponents of Nordic-style democratic socialism would argue that, yes, the Nordic countries do have higher unemployment rates than the United States. But surely the difference isn't that large. They would be right, according to official records. But let's keep in mind that Nordic welfare states are hiding much of the true unemployment.

The previously quoted report from McKinsey discusses the prevalence of hidden unemployment. There we can read that the official unemployment in Sweden was somewhat above 5 percent in 2004. This figure was, however, quite misleading. Much of the true unemployment was hidden by the government through various public labor market programs and by excluding unemployed people from the labor force statistics. When including those in hidden unemployment, McKinsey found that the total unemployment figure was around 17 percent.[26] The previous year another, similar report had been written, by analyst Jan Edling. Edling estimated that since the beginning of the 1990s, approximately one-fifth of the Swedish population of working age has been supported by unemployment benefits, sick leave benefits, or early retirement benefits. Now, what is interesting is that Edling was no critique of social democracy. Rather, he was working as an analyst for the Swedish Trade Union Confederation LO. The confederation is the heart of the Swedish labor movement and has very close ties to the Swedish Social Democratic party, which at the time controlled the government. LO refused to publish the report, believing it to be critical of the government in particular and the social democratic welfare model in general. Edling quit his job in protest and made the material publicly available.[27]

Other studies have since supported Edling's findings about high levels of hidden unemployment.[28] Perhaps the most interesting one is that which was coauthored by Swedish economist Lars Ljungqvist together with Thomas Sargent. Thomas Sargent is one of the most well-cited economists in the world, and was in 2011 awarded with the Nobel Prize in Economics. The two economists calculated the real underlying rate of unemployment in Sweden. By using historic data they were able to sort out how much of sick leave, early retirement, and other forms of labor market exclusion was due to normal factors, such as people being too ill to work, and how much the welfare system was hiding the true employment level.[29] In 2014 economist Susanne Spector published a study in which she had updated Sargent and Ljuhgqvist's measure with new data. There we could see that the true unemployment level in Sweden has varied between 14 and 18 percent since the mid-1990s.[30]

It is not a right-wing conspiracy idea that the Swedish welfare state hides unemployment.

Although estimates do differ somewhat, the various economists who have looked at the unemployment level in the Swedish welfare agree on one thing: the true level is much higher than official figures. It is not a right-wing conspiracy idea that the Swedish welfare state hides unemployment, but rather, a fact shown by the analysis performed within the labor movement itself and by one of the leading economists in the world. The picture is quite similar in other parts of the Nordics. As will be discussed in the next part of this book, not least the Norwegian welfare state—which has remained generous thanks to massive oil wealth while other Nordic states have scaled back their welfare state in recent years—is trapping many families in hidden unemployment.

Once we take a closer look, the myth of Nordic countries being able to defy economic logic is easy to bust. These countries had a phenomenal economic growth when they had small governments and free markets. As they moved toward socialism, entrepreneurship, growing prosperity and new jobs all came to a halt. A shift back to free markets brought back growth. Still today we can observe that the large welfare states are creating, and hiding, unemployment. Of course, this isn't necessarily a case for Nordic-style welfare states being a generally bad idea. One could always argue that there is an inherent value in combining high taxes with generous welfare programs. Slower growth and higher labor market exclusion might be seen by some as a price worth paying for having a large welfare state. Most admirers of Nordic-style democratic socialism, however, do not follow this line of argument. Instead, they cling to the false notion that Nordic countries are bumblebees that prove that socialism doesn't have negative effects on the economy.

This is simply not the case. The laws of the economic universe exist in Denmark, Sweden, Finland, and Norway. And they work much as they do in America.

7

WHY ARE SO FEW NORDIC WOMEN AT THE TOP?

WE LIVE IN AN AGE of women's progress. Or to be more precise, we live in an age when a number of long-term trends are paving the way for women to climb the career ladder around the world. One such trend is that norms are changing. It is still common to find gender-biased attitudes wherein individuals are seen as less competent, reliable, or valuable simply because they are women. However, over time, such attitudes have become less widespread. Recent surveys, for example, have found that the majority of Americans believe that women are every bit as capable of being corporate and political leaders as men.[1]

While women's progress is very much a global phenomenon, there can't be any doubt that one region of the world is leading in gender equality—the Nordics. *The Global Gender Gap* report concludes that "the Nordic nations continue to act as role models in terms of their ability to achieve gender parity."[2] Saadia Zahidi, senior director and head of gender parity and human capital at the World Economic Forum, has this to say about gender equality in the region: "While patterns vary across the Nordic countries, on the whole, these economies have made it possible for parents to combine work and family, resulting in more women in the workplace, more shared participation in childcare, more equitable distribution of labor at home, better work-life balance for both women and men and, in some cases, a boost to waning fertility rates."[3]

International praise of Nordic gender equality is easy to find. Katrin Bennhold at the *New York Times*, for example, argues that Sweden's feminist model is beneficial both to men and women in tearing down traditional gender roles: "In this land of Viking lore, men are at the heart of the gender-equality debate. The ponytailed center-right finance minister calls himself a feminist, ads for cleaning products rarely feature women as homemakers, and preschools vet books for gender stereotypes in animal characters. For nearly four decades, governments of all political hues have legislated to give women equal rights at work—and men equal rights at home." Like many other international proponents of Nordic gender equality, Bennhold admires the "social engineering" that has made it possible for "a new definition of masculinity" to emerge. She also wrote enthusiastically about "laws reserving at least two months of the generously paid, thirteen-month parental leave exclusively for fathers" and other features of Nordic welfare states, which are said to have "set off profound social change."[4]

Those who follow international news sources are routinely given the impression that Nordic gender egalitarianism simply results from the social democratic welfare state policies introduced in this part of the world. Through social engineering, the social democrats have shaped their citizens into gender-equal beings. The British left-of-center newspaper the *Guardian*, for example, informs its readers: "Official figures from Eurostat show that 77% of women in Sweden had a job in 2014—the highest level in the European Union. Children are guaranteed a place in childcare from the age of 12 months for a very modest sum, making it possible for women to return to work."[5] On the *Guardian*'s web page, this news item directly links to an opinion column by Gabrielle Jackson. The article is entitled "Force men to take paternity leave. It will make the world a better place." It, of course, argues that the Swedish model with a welfare state providing generous paternity leave is a fantastic solution.[6]

So, Nordic-style social democracy is the best way of promoting women's careers? There is indeed a case to be made for this argument. Several aspects of Nordic welfare states—such as public provision of child care, generous parental leave, and liberal sick leave—are aimed at making the combination of work and family easier for parents, and particularly so for mothers. However, the reality is more complex than what admirers of social democracy might believe. To begin with, it is certainly true that the Nordic countries, and Sweden in particular, are role models in gender equality. But this success did not materialize with the welfare state. Rather, Nordic gender equality stretches back many centuries before the foundation of modern welfare systems.

Much as portrayed in TV series such as HBO's *Vikings*, ancient Norse societies were already quite gender equal.

Much as portrayed in TV series such as HBO's *Vikings*, ancient Norse societies were already quite gender equal. Women had considerably more influence than in other contemporary cultures. As an illustration, Scandinavian folklore is primarily focused on men who venture on longboats to trade, explore, and pillage. Yet the folklore also includes shieldmaidens, women chosen to fight as warriors. John Skylitzes, a Greek historian of the late eleventh century, documented that women were indeed participating in Norse armies. This came as something of a shock to the enemies of the Vikings.[7] The fact that women were allowed to carry arms, and train as warriors, suggests that gender-segmentation of early Norse societies was considerably more lax—or at least more flexible—than in other parts of contemporary Europe.

Evidence also indicates that women in early Nordic societies could inherit land and property, keep control over their dowry in marriage, and control a third of the property they shared with their spouses. In addition, they could—under some circumstances, at least—"participate in the public sphere on the same level as men." Medieval law, which likely reflects earlier traditions, supports this notion. Medieval inheritance laws in Norway followed family relations through both male and female lines. Additionally, women could opt for a divorce.[8] These rights might not seem impressive today, but were rather unusual in a historic context. In many contemporary European and Asian societies, the view was that women simply belonged to their fathers or husbands, having little rights to property, divorce, or inclusion in the public sphere.

Nordic gender egalitarianism continued after the Viking age, particularly in Sweden. In much of the world, women were excluded from participating, at least fully, in the rise of early capitalism during the eighteenth and nineteenth centuries. In essence, free markets and property rights were institutions for men, not women. Although Sweden and the other Nordic countries were far from completely egalitarian, they challenged contemporary gender norms by opening up early capitalism for women's participation. In 1798 married women in Sweden were given legal majority and juridical responsibility within the affairs of their businesses. At the time, this was a highly unusual practice. As a comparison, the state of Maine was groundbreaking in allowing women to own and manage property in 1821, but only under the condition that their spouses were incapacitated. Massachusetts and Tennessee introduced the same legislation in 1835, with other states gradually following suit. Swedish author Anders Johnson, who has written numerous books about the development of business freedom, explains that women in Sweden during the first half of the nineteenth century had more opportunities to run businesses than in other parts of Europe.[9]

Nordic policies continued to be friendly to women's work participation in the beginning of the twentieth century. For example, around 1900 the question of protective labor legislation was brought up in the Nordic countries. Inspired by international developments, governments wanted to "protect" women from work in factories. These proposals caused a heated debate. Sweden did introduce a night-work prohibition in 1909, after considerable criticism from the women's movement. Unlike in other European countries and the United States, a special prohibition on women's night work was, however, never included in Danish and Norwegian factory laws. Women were allowed to participate in the industrial upheaval of these countries.[10]

A perhaps unintentional effect of the transition toward welfare state monopolies was that women's business ownership suffered.

Anita Lignell Du Rietz has written numerous studies on women's business ownership in Sweden over time. She has shown that many businesses, such as taverns, tailor stores, breweries, and shops were run by women entrepreneurs during the nineteenth century. Other women-dominated businesses that developed over time included schools and pharmacies. However, as the Swedish welfare state grew during the twentieth century, government monopolies were enforced, crowding out private enterprise. Crucially, male-dominated sectors, such as manufacturing, mining, and forestry, continued to be run by private firms. On the other hand, women-dominated sectors, such as health care, child care, and education, were taken over by the public sector. Therefore, a perhaps unintentional effect of the transition toward welfare state monopolies was that women's business ownership suffered.[11] In fact, the development of the welfare state—although aimed at fostering gender equality and successful in boosting women's labor participations—has limited women's progress in many ways.

Today, at first glance, Nordic countries seem to have all that is required for women to thrive in the workplace; they have high rates of employment among women, uniquely gender-equal norms, public provision of child care, and generous parental leave programs. It might thus come as a surprise that Nordic countries have relatively few women in management. According to the International Labor Organization, the share of women managers in the Nordics is far below that in the United States. Iceland, the Nordic country with a more limited welfare model, is the only one that comes close (see the following table[12]).

SHARE OF WOMEN MANAGERS

COUNTRY	PERCENT OF ALL MANAGERS (THROUGH 2012)
UNITED STATES	43
ICELAND	40
SWEDEN	36
NORWAY	32
FINLAND	30
DENMARK	28

International Labour Organization (2015).

It may come as a surprise to American admirers of Nordic-style democratic socialism that these countries have a systematic underrepresentation of women at the top. Although few seem aware of this fact, it has for long been evident that these countries have lower shares of women reaching top business careers than in many other modern economies. A Eurostat study from 1995 found that the share of women among top earners was only 6 percent in Sweden, considerably lower than the 15 percent in France.[13] Nine years later a study from UCLA concluded that merely 11 percent of managers and professionals in Sweden were women, lower than in other developed economies.[14] How is it that the country with the most gender-equal norms, and an astonishing history of gender equality, underperforms in this regard? Why do we see that the Nordic region as a whole, although having a number of advantages both in terms of policy and gender-equal values, performs so badly?

This seems even more puzzling once we take into account that politicians from both left and right in the Nordics put great emphasis on feminist ideas. Sweden is again one step ahead of the pack. The former Communist Party leader Gudrun Schyman has built up a strong, left-oriented feminist party in the country. The Swedish Feminist Initiative, as the party is called, made international headlines when it won a seat in the European Parliament during the 2014 election. The same year, the Feminist Initiative gained 3.1 percent of votes during the Swedish national election, close to the 4.0 percent limit for entering parliament. This is quite impressive in a country where the mainstream parties are already competing for the feminist vote.

In Sweden a gender perspective, built in part on the idea that gender is a social construct and that there is a classical Marxist struggle between the sexes, underpins much of academic research into women's issues as well as the political debate. Gender theory is part of the public education system, from kindergarten to doctorate level studies. All this seems to do little, if anything, to pave the way for women's career opportunities in the modern marketplace. Clearly, it cannot be a lack of feminist ideas and policies, welfare state support, or gender-equal values that is holding the country back compared to the rest of the world. Of course, one could argue that Sweden could have even more of left-oriented feminism, even more welfare state support for working mothers, and even more gender-equal values. But already the country is ahead of the rest of the world in these regards. Why, then, do we find few women who climb to the top of the private sector? There must be an explanation, for

Sweden in particular and for the Nordic region as a whole, for why women are held back.

Economists Magnus Henrekson and Mikael Stenkula have written a scientific review titled "Why Are There So Few Female Top Executives in Egalitarian Welfare States?" They note that Sweden, where women have made considerable progress in society as a whole, are clearly underrepresented in executive positions. Even when public-sector executives are included, which inflates the Swedish share of women on top, Sweden has few women executives. The two economists wrote, "Sweden falls behind not only Anglo-Saxon countries, such as the United States and the United Kingdom, but also other large continental European countries, such as West Germany and France [in terms of share of women in intermediate and higher executive positions]. Among the countries compared, Sweden clearly comes out at the bottom." Henrekson and Stenkula conclude that "broad-based welfare-state policies impede women's representation in elite competitive positions."[15]

Similarly, Monica Renstig, founder of Women's Business Research Institute in Sweden wrote:

Which country is most likely to foster female managers to reach the highest rungs of power? Would you say it is the US where new mothers are offered 12 weeks of maternity leave, almost no subsidized child care, no paid paternity leave and where there is a notoriously hard-driving business culture? Or Sweden, where new moms and dads have 14 months of fully paid time-off at their jobs? The correct answer is the United States. Despite the fact that Sweden has put great effort into building up its welfare system in the hopes of providing women with more opportunity to have children and a career, in the private sector, few women are breaking the glass ceiling.[16]

Interestingly enough, the notion that welfare-state policies can limit women's ability to reach the top is not new. Going back a few years to 1998, a report entitled *Gender and Jobs: Sex Segregation of Occupations in the World*, published by the International Labour Office noted that an unusually gender segregated labor market had developed in Nordic countries, since many women worked in the public rather than the private sector. The report found that "in terms of differences among industrialized countries, several studies comment on how *Nordic Scandinavian countries, and in particular Sweden, have among the greatest inequalities.*"[17]

A key explanation lies in the nature of the welfare state. In Sweden and other Nordic countries, female-dominated sectors, such as health care and education, are mainly run by the public sector. A study from the Nordic Innovation Centre, for example, explains: "Nearly 50 percent of all women employees in Denmark are employed in the public sector. Compared to the male counterpart where just above 15 percent are employed in the public sector. This difference alone can explain some of the gender gap with respect to entrepreneurship. The same story is prevalent in Sweden."[18]

Similarly, Matti Alestalo, Sven E. O. Hort, and Stein Kuhnle wrote in their paper *The Nordic Model: Conditions, Origins, Outcomes, Lessons*:

The Nordic countries deviated from other advanced countries because the expansion of the service sector was mainly a welfare state phenomenon. The increasing female labour force participation was paved by the expansion of public employment. Also in this respect Sweden was the leader, followed by Denmark, while Finland and Norway stayed at [a] somewhat lower level. In Sweden, Denmark and Norway a great proportion of this change came through the increase of part-time work but the fate of Finnish women was full-time work.[19]

The emergence of a large public sector has historically played an important role for women's entry into the labor market. One reason is that many women have found jobs in the public sector; another is that public services such as child care facilitate the combination of work and the fulfillment of family responsibilities. The expansion of the public sector, not least that of public child care, in part explains why the Nordic nations reached a high employment rate among women earlier than other Western countries. Still today the Nordics have many women in employment. In the long run, however, women's career success has been hampered by the fact that the labor market entry of women has been so intimately connected with the growth of the public sector. Public-sector monopolies have harmed women's progress.

Lack of competition and public-sector monopolies tend to limit long-term productive growth.[20] In addition, monopolistic employers have limited incentives to treat their employees well. This doesn't only apply to the Nordics, but also to other countries where the government runs services such as education and health care. If you are a nurse in the United Kingdom and are displeased with how the National Health Service is treating you, what other employer can you turn to? If you are a teacher in the United States, in a time before voucher schools were allowed, who could you turn to if dissatisfied with how public schools were run? These issues are quite relevant for women's progress in the Nordic countries, where the public sector is large. Monopolistic structures have combined with a strong influence of union wage setting to create a situation where individual hard work is not rewarded significantly. Wages in the women-dominated public sectors in Nordic countries are flat. Wage rises follow seniority, according to labor union contracts, rather than individual achievement. There are, of course, managerial positions also in the public sector, but the opportunities for individual career paths, and certainly for entrepreneurship, are typically more limited compared with in the private sector.

Eva Meyersson Milgrom, Trond Petersen, and Vemund Snartland have looked at the wage differences between men and women in Sweden, Norway, and the United States. They found that "the wage gap is small when comparing men and women working in the same type of occupation for the same employer. Segregation of men and women by occupation accounts for more of the gap in Sweden than in the other two countries."[21] Thus, it seems that the occupation segregation in Sweden—closely connected with public-sector monopolies is creating distinct disadvantages for working women.

Women make up around 70 percent of those in the various Nordic countries working in the public sector. This is higher than the average rate of below 60 percent for modern economies.[22] It should also be kept in mind that women in Nordic countries tend to be particularly overrepresented in local public-sector jobs, where the pay and career progress is more limited compared with the state sector. In Sweden, for example, central government jobs, which tend to be better paying, are evenly divided between men and women, while only one-fifth of those in local government employment are men.[23]

The notion that public sector monopolies hinder women can be studied more in depth by looking at the change brought on by recent liberalizations. Gradually since the early 1990s, the previous public monopolies have been opened up in Sweden as voucher systems, allowing for-profit schools, hospitals, and elderly care centers to operate with tax funding. A study from the Confederation of Swedish Enterprise has looked at how incomes have developed for the individuals who worked for public-sector employers in welfare, and whose workplaces were privatized during 2002. Privatization drove up wages, evident by the fact that these individuals gained 5 percentage points' higher wages than similar employees whose workplaces had not been privatized. Individuals whose workplaces become privatized also benefited from gaining a stronger foothold on the labor market. Their risk of being unemployed was lower than those whose workplaces had continued to be part of public monopolies.[24]

Again we see that the Nordic countries are illustrative of the benefits that come from market reforms. But of course, those who point to Nordic-style democratic socialism as the recipe for gender equality tend to overlook how scaling back the scope of government has promoted women's careers. Instead they admire the state-mandated quotas that were introduced in Norway in 2006. The law, which requires that 40 percent of board members of public companies be women, is often held up internationally as a feminist success story. The simple line of reasoning seems to be: the quotas aimed to increase the share of women on corporate boards, and achieved this goal. In reality however, the policies have been anything but a success. To begin with, researchers have found that the quotas have been bad for business. A sign that the quota law was not popular among the business community is that share prices fell on average by 3.5 percent following its announcement. Once firms were forced to follow the law, another challenge became apparent: the difficulty to fill the board positions with experienced individuals. The new female directors were on average eight years younger than existing male directors, which suggests less experience.[25]

Kenneth Ahern and Amy Dittmar have examined the Norwegian evidence by looking not only at the stock price but also the Tobin's Q. This measure is a commonly used way of examining the market value of firms. The researchers found that firm value as measured by Tobin's Q fell by over 12 percent with every 10 percent increase in female board members. They wrote, "The quota led to younger and less experienced boards, increases in leverage and acquisitions, and deterioration in operating performance."[26] More important, the affirmative action legislation has systematically failed to improve women's career potential. Marianne Bertrand and her coauthors have looked at how introduction of gender quotas affected women in Norwegian firms. They found the following:

- There was no trickle-down effect. This means that while a few women on top gained higher wages due to affirmative action directly benefiting them, the broad group of women employees did not receive higher wages due to a gender shift in board leadership.

- The reform had "no obvious impact on highly qualified women whose qualifications mirror those of board members but who were not appointed to boards." The affirmative action thus failed to break the glass ceiling in any meaningful way except for benefiting a few elite women.

- There were no significant changes in the gender wage gap or in female representation in top positions. Again, women's wages and the ability of women in general to climb to the top were simply not affected.

- Lastly, "there is little evidence that the reform affected the decisions of women more generally; it was not accompanied by any change in female enrollment in business education programs, or a convergence in earnings trajectories between recent male and female graduates of such programs. While young women preparing for a career in business report being aware of the reform and expect their earnings and promotion chances to benefit from it, the reform did not affect their fertility and marital plans."[27]

As another example, in mid-2015 the *Nordic Labour Journal* published an article explaining that Norway had no female CEOs in its sixty largest firms, even though eight years had passed since the quotas had been introduced.[28] Norway thus seems to be the perfect case for why affirmative action is not a good idea if we want to promote women's career opportunities. It is quite typical that global admirers of social democracy draw the precisely opposite conclusion. Facts about the Nordics seem less interesting than the myths of successful socialism in the region. Separating culture from politics is again important.

There are indeed good reasons to admire the Nordic countries for their women-friendly attitudes, history, and perhaps also family-oriented policies. But it is evident that the social democratic system, as well as affirmative action, have been largely unsuccessful in promoting women's ability to climb to the top. In this regard, the American system seems much more women-friendly than the Nordic one.

> The social democratic system, as well as affirmative action, have been largely unsuccessful in promoting women's ability to climb to the top.

Part 4

WELFARE POVERTY

8

THE GENEROUS WELFARE TRAP

BY LAUNCHING THE NEW DEAL, Franklin D. Roosevelt became the architect of the American welfare state. However, Roosevelt was concerned that the institution he was fostering would not live long, since it might destroy the spirit of self-reliance. Two years into his presidency, he held a speech to Congress praising the expansion of welfare programs. During the same speech the president warned that many of the individuals who had lost their jobs during the Great Depression still remained unemployed. "The burden on the Federal Government has grown with great rapidity," he said, adding that one reason was that many had become dependent on various forms of public handouts. With foresight Roosevelt explained: "When humane considerations are concerned, Americans give them precedence. The lessons of history, confirmed by the evidence immediately before me, show conclusively that continued dependence upon relief induces a spiritual and moral disintegration fundamentally destructive to the national fibre. To dole out relief in this way is to administer a narcotic, a subtle destroyer of the human spirit. It is inimical to the dictates of sound policy. It is in violation of the traditions of America."[1] In today's political climate, Franklin D. Roosevelt's view on public benefits would seem quite harsh, far from politically correct. Hillary Clinton and Bernie Sanders would never say such things. Most Republican candidates wouldn't either. Roosevelt's words today sound like something coming from a radical opponent of the American welfare state. Many would surely be surprised to find that they were uttered by the founder of the very same system.

> "To dole out relief in this way is to administer a narcotic. . . .
>
> It is in violation of the traditions of America." —PRESIDENT
>
> FRANKLIN D. ROOSEVELT, 1935

Going back in time, the views of Roosevelt were anything but uncommon. In the beginning of the twentieth century, even the proponents of the welfare state were greatly worried that the build-up of welfare programs might endanger the social fabric. To understand this reasoning, we must bear in mind that for the welfare state to function properly, it is not enough that most individuals follow the norm of properly paying their taxes. Neither is it enough that most individuals follow the norm of not overusing welfare services. Rather, for the system to work in the long term, the vast majority must abide the social contract. From the individual perspective, as transfer schemes become more generous and taxes are raised, it becomes increasingly lucrative to sideline the social contract. If government hand-outs are a good source of income, why work hard for a living? If taxes have become too high, why not try to dodge them? When all individuals in society follow the norms of working hard, paying taxes, and only using welfare programs when in need, the system will function properly even with a generous welfare system. However, if a critical mass of people change their behavior, the erosion of welfare norms can accelerate as the social contract falls apart.[2]

Group psychology plays a key role in society. According to researchers Fehr and Urs Fischbacher, legal rules and legal enforcement mechanisms typically lack effectiveness if not backed up by social norms. That is to say, we follow the rules when most of us think they make sense. In free societies governments don't really have the power of enforcing rules that fundamentally go against the beliefs of the people. Social norms can in this sense be seen as rules of "conditional cooperation." Critically, "defection of others is a legitimate excuse for individual defection."[3] In other words, if an individual perceives that her neighbors stick to the norm, she will be likely to do the same. If the neighbor is dodging his taxes or cheating the system to get money from the government, however, the individual's own tendency to follow the rules will be diminished. Why work hard to pay for the neighbor to slack off? An erosion of the conditional cooperation underlying the welfare state can have grave societal effects. The result can be deteriorating working ethics, increased public dependency, and social tension.

To further complicate the matter, it is not enough to implement stricter enforcement of rules. Government measures to control how much public programs are used might signal to law-abiding citizens that violations have become a common practice. Friedrich Heinemann is a German scholar who has studied how generous welfare systems over time can undermine the very same norms that make the welfare systems possible to uphold. Heinemann explains that government sanctions can "be perceived as limiting citizens' self-determination and will then further crowd out the intrinsic motivation to respect the law."[4] This means that if society reaches a point where overutilization of welfare programs becomes common practice, the deterioration of norms might prove difficult to stop. Politicians cannot simply repair the social fabric through public dictates. In this light, one can better understand how Roosevelt himself viewed doling out relief as "a narcotic, a subtle destroyer of the human spirit." While the president actively expanded the American welfare state, he wanted to point out that there were legitimate reasons for concern about welfare dependency.

Over time, proponents of large public sectors forgot the warning words of Roosevelt and other early welfare state architects. They grew more confident that generous government services and handouts could in fact be introduced and funded by high tax rates, without the moral fiber of society suffering in the process. An important reason is that advocates of welfare policy pointed to northern Europe and claimed that the development in this region proved that social democratic policies could be combined with strong working ethics. If the Nordic countries could have generous welfare, why couldn't America? The evidence from America itself pointed in the opposite conclusion. As Ronald Reagan explained during a radio address in 1986, it was quite evident that welfare dependency was a genuine concern. Reagan, who was serving his second term as president, said:

From the 1950s on, poverty in America was declining. American society, an opportunity society, was doing its wonders. Economic growth was providing a ladder for millions to climb up out of poverty and into prosperity. In 1964 the famous War on Poverty was declared and a funny thing happened. Poverty, as measured by dependency, stopped shrinking and then actually began to grow worse. I guess you could say, poverty won the war. Poverty won in part because instead of helping the poor, government programs ruptured the bonds holding poor families together.[5]

"Government programs ruptured the bonds holding poor families together." —President Ronald Reagan, 1986

The president continued to provide a textbook example of how families can be adversely affected by welfare programs intended to help them:

Perhaps the most insidious effect of welfare is its usurpation of the role of provider. In States where payments are highest, for instance, public assistance for a single mother can amount to much more than the usable income of a minimum wage job. In other words, it can pay for her to quit work. Many families are eligible for substantially higher benefits when the father is not present. What must it do to a man to know that his own children will be better off if he is never legally recognized as their father? Under existing welfare rules, a teenage girl who becomes pregnant can make herself eligible for welfare benefits that will set her up in an apartment of her own, provide medical care, and feed and clothe her. She only has to fulfill one condition—not marry or identify the father.[6]

Ronald Reagan's critique resonated with the people. The American public supported policies to limit the scope of welfare programs. Not only small-government Republicans and Libertarians, but also Democrats, such as Bill Clinton, continued to raise concern about how overly generous welfare programs—although introduced with noble intentions—could erode personal responsibility and disrupt family structures. The same issue has been highly relevant in many other parts of the world. Yet there has been a persistent conviction among the modern proponents of welfare states that it is indeed—somehow—possible to create stable systems with generous benefits and high taxes. The main line of reasoning is based on the Nordics. The welfare states in this part of the world seem to, at least at first glance, succeed in providing extensive services and generous cash benefits without eroding personal responsibility. If generous welfare works in Sweden and Denmark, why not also in the rest of the world?

Previously mentioned German researcher Friedrich Heinemann has set about examining whether Roosevelt's warning "of the moral disintegration effect of welfare dependency" is really something to be worried about. By looking at the World Value Survey, a global survey of attitudes conducted since the early 1980s, Heinemann has concluded that a self-destructive mechanism exists in a welfare state. When welfare becomes more generous, and when unemployment reaches high levels, people find it more acceptable to take advantage of welfare programs: "In the long-run an increase of government benefits and unemployment is associated with deteriorating welfare state ethics."[7] Basically, people react as we would expect them to react. If government handouts become generous, more people will seek them. Particularly when jobs are scarce, welfare dependency therefore becomes a real concern.

Interestingly, the World Value Survey shows that erosion of norms is very much a thing in the Nordics. In the beginning of the 1980s, 82 percent of Swedes and 80 percent of Norwegians agreed with the statement "Claiming government benefits to which you are not entitled is never justifiable." We shouldn't be surprised that benefit morale was strong in this part of the world. After all, as we read previously in this book, the Nordic people had over generations adopted a culture with strong emphasis on hard work, individual responsibility, social cohesion, and trust. However, as the population adjusted their behavior to new economic policies, benefit morale dropped steadily. In the survey conducted between 2005 and 2008, only 56 percent of Norwegians and 61 percent of Swedes believed that it was never right to claim benefits to which they were not entitled. The survey conducted between 2010 and 2014 only included Sweden out of the Nordic countries. It found that benefit morale had continued to fall, as merely 55 percent of Swedes answered that it was never right to overuse benefits.[8]

The thing with norms is that they change slowly, over the course of generations. When the government raises taxes or makes living on benefits more advantageous, most people continue to act as they have done previously. But this does not mean that norms are set in stone. Over time even the Nordic people have changed their attitudes as social democratic policies have made it less rewarding to work hard and more rewarding to live off the government. This is in accordance with research by French economist Jean-Baptiste Michau. He has suggested that a link exists between government benefits and cultural transmissions of work ethics. Michau explains that parents make rational choices regarding "how much effort to exert to raise their children to work hard," based on their "expectations on the policy that will be implemented by the next generation." Therefore, changes in culture happen over time as families react to new policies. Once Michau takes into account that changes occur slowly, he can show that generous unemployment insurance benefits can explain much of the changes in unemployment levels in Europe that have occurred over time.[9]

The idea of a self-destructive welfare state [is] something that serious researchers have found support for.

In another study Martin Halla, Mario Lackner, and Friedrich G. Schneider performed an empirical analysis of the dynamics of the welfare state. They explained that individuals do not respond to changes in economic incentives right away, because people are constrained by social norms for some time: "therefore, the disincentive effects may materialize only with considerable time lags." This is to say, if your parents teach you to never live off welfare benefits if not forced to, you are likely to follow this norm even if the benefits become more generous. When the generosity of the system increases, however, parents become less likely to teach this norm to their children. The shift in behavior thus takes some time to occur. Interestingly, the authors found that in the short term, increased government spending on welfare programs can even have a small positive influence on benefit morale. As the welfare state is expanded, at least some people seem to make a concerted effort in not overusing it. Perhaps some even convince their neighbors to do the same. However, after some time the expansion of welfare programs leads to a deterioration of benefit morale. The three researchers concluded that "the welfare state destroys its own (economic) foundation and we have to approve the hypothesis of the self-destructive welfare state."[10] The idea of a self-destructive welfare state might sound like something thought up by right-wing conspiracy theorists but is in reality something that serious researchers have found support for.

The theory of the self-destructive dynamics of welfare states has to a large degree been developed by Assar Lindbeck, one of Sweden's leading modern economists. Lindbeck has stated that changes in work ethics are related to a rising dependence on welfare state institutions.[11] Additionally, he points out that the evidence of explicit benefit fraud in Sweden leads to a weakening of norms against overusing various benefit systems. An example is that you find out that your neighbor is receiving sick-pay benefits, while also having an under-the-table job, or black-sector job. The knowledge that he is cheating the system might encourage you to follow suit. According to Lindbeck, reforms to limit fraud are therefore quite important for maintaining a welfare state.[12]

A number of attitude studies in Sweden reach the same conclusion: a significant portion of the population has come to consider that it is acceptable to live off sickness benefits without actually being sick. A survey from 2001, for example, showed that four out of ten Swedish employees believed it was acceptable for those who were not sick but who felt stressed at work to claim sickness benefit. Additionally, almost half of those surveyed answered that it was acceptable for employees to claim sickness benefits if they were dissatisfied with their working environments or had problems within their families.[13] Other Swedish studies have pointed to increases in sickness absence during sports events. For instance, absence due to sickness increased by almost 7 percent among men at the time of the Winter Olympics in 1988, and by 16 percent in connection with TV broadcasts of the World Championship in cross-country skiing in 1987.[14] During the 2002 soccer World Cup, the increase in sickness absence among men was an astonishing 41 percent. The stark difference between the events during the end of the 1980s and the beginning of the 2000s might be seen as an indication of the deterioration of work ethics over time, during a period when the population became adjusted to generous sick-leave entitlements.[15]

During recent years, governments on both the right and the left in Sweden have reduced the generosity of the welfare system. Strict controls have been introduced in the sick leave system and other welfare programs. A recent paper suggests that the reforms may need to be even more far reaching to reverse the long-term effect that the welfare state has had on people's behaviors. Economist Martin Ljunge has written: "Younger generations use sickness insurance more often than older generations. Amongst the younger generation twenty percentage points more take a sick leave day compared with those born twenty years before, after other circumstances have been adjusted for. The higher demand for sick leave pay amongst the younger generations can be seen as a measure of how rapidly the welfare state affects attitudes towards the use of public benefits." Behind the technical scientific language, we find a strong message: generous welfare programs can have a long-lasting effect on people's behavior by encouraging overreliance on public support. Even many years after public benefits have been changed, people's norms still keep changing as they become adjusted to generous welfare.[16]

"Much evidence suggests that the welfare state also has a very costly and long-lasting effect on the working ethic of Danes."—DANISH ECONOMIST CASPER HUNNERUP DAHL

Similarly, Danish researcher Casper Hunnerup Dahl has concluded: "The high degree of distribution in the Danish welfare state does not merely reduce the concrete incentives that some Danes have for taking a job or to work extra in the job that one already holds. Much evidence suggests that the welfare state also has a very costly and long-lasting effect on the working ethic of Danes."[17] There can be little doubt, then, that the erosion of norms due to long-term adaptation to welfare policy is an observable phenomenon rather than just theory. Roosevelt and Reagan were right, and those who believe that generous welfare does not erode norms are wrong.

For the outside world the Nordic countries are still today shining examples of how large public sectors can be introduced without the moral hazard of welfare policy. However, much of the policy debate during recent years in the Nordic countries themselves has been about how to deal with overutilization and deteriorating norms. Sweden has already cut down considerably on the generosity of public services and welfare transfers, at the same time reducing the taxes on work significantly. Denmark has seen a slower pace of reform. However, the Danes are quite aware that change is needed. Somewhat surprisingly, it is not only the conservatives or libertarians in Denmark who raise the issue of dependency on government handouts. The Danish Social Democrats themselves actively acknowledge this problem.

Bjarne Corydon, who served as the country's Social Democrat finance minister at the time, made international headlines in 2013 by pointing to the need to reduce the generosity of transfer systems in Denmark. Corydon explained that it was no mere coincidence that the government was reforming taxes, welfare aid, and the system for early retirement: "The truth is that we are in full swing with a dramatically positive agenda, which is about strengthening and modernizing the welfare state, and the result of the change will be a much better society than the one we have today." The leading social democrat went as far as formulating a new vision for the future of the welfare state: "I believe in the competition state as the modern welfare state. If we are to ensure support for the welfare state, we must focus on the quality of public services rather than transfer payments."[18] Denmark is today often held up as a utopian society by the American Left. How many are aware that the politicians on the left in the very same country are openly criticizing the idea of overly generous welfare programs?

"I believe in the competition state as the modern welfare state." —BJARNE CORYDON, FORMER SOCIAL DEMOCRAT FINANCE MINISTER OF DENMARK

Americans who still believe the moral risk of generous welfare can be avoided would do themselves a service by reading (with the help of Google Translate perhaps) a report published by the previous Social Democrat government of Denmark. The report calculated that 400,000 Danish citizens had few economic incentives to participate in the labor market. These individuals lost 80 percent or more of their incomes when starting work, since they forfeited benefits and had to pay taxes. Through extensive reforms of taxes and benefits, the government hoped to reduce the number to 250,000 individuals. Even the lower number represents around one in ten among the working-age population of the small country.[19] In June 2015 the Danish left-of-center government lost the election to a new right-of-center coalition, which has an even greater emphasis on welfare reform. Interestingly the Social Democrats themselves increased their support in the election, regaining the position as the country's largest party. Power shifted since the coalition partners of the Social Democrats, who want to keep generous welfare benefits, lost considerable voter support. The Danish people thus rewarded the parties on both the right and the left who wanted to reduce the generosity of welfare programs. Perhaps they realized that when it comes to welfare state policy, sometimes less is more.

Other northern European welfare states have followed a similar path as Denmark and Sweden. The Netherlands long had one of the most generous welfare systems in the world. During the beginning of the 1980s the country ranked as a top spender in terms of welfare policy, on par with the (at the time) famously generous Swedish welfare state. Since then, however, it has scaled back its welfare systems, reduced the scope of public spending, privatized social security, and introduced elaborate market mechanisms in the provision of health care and social protection.[20] Although not geographically a part of Scandinavia, the Netherlands has very similar cultural, economic, and political features as its northern neighbors. A difference is that the Dutch were earlier in shifting away from a very generous welfare system to a more limited model. The ambition to provide social safety nets, health care, and schooling to its underprivileged citizens has remained. However, by scaling down the generosity of the system, and creating insurance markets that combine universal coverage with competition and individual responsibility, the Dutch have found a new welfare model. Arguably, this more scaled-down model is more durable, since it encourages individual responsibility.

Germany and Finland have never introduced welfare regimes quite as ambitious as Denmark's and Sweden's, but they have worked to reduce welfare dependency. The United Kingdom, which has an even more limited welfare model, is also interesting to look at. The British have had less generous welfare state benefits than their Nordic neighbors. At the same time, they have lacked the Nordic culture of success. Therefore, the social challenges relating to welfare dependency are quite evident in British society. An extensive debate has for some years now been raging in the country about the need to restrengthen norms. In the beginning of 2014, for example, the documentary series *Benefit Street* was aired and ran for five episodes. It showed the lives of residents of James Turner Street in Birmingham, where reportedly 90 percent of residents claim benefit. The reality series sparked a massive debate about benefit claims and how the British welfare model creates a lack of motivation to seek employment. Although the program was criticized by the Left, recent political trends indicate that the route to welfare reform is favored by many among the British general public.[21] When you think about it, isn't it curious that American admirers of large welfare states so seldom point to the United Kingdom as a role model? After all, the United States was founded as a British colony and has to this day much deeper cultural links to the UK than to the Nordics. Arguably, the development shown in Benefit Street is very close to what Ronald Reagan and other American critiques of overly generous public transfer systems have been pointing to.

There is a possible exception to the new welfare contract being formulated in northern European welfare states: Norway. Thanks to its massive oil wealth in the Atlantic Ocean, this mountainous country has retained the social democrat ideal of very generous public programs. However, as Roosevelt so eloquently put it, welfare dependency is not only an economic but also a human issue. Certainly the oil funds have made it possible for Norway to afford paying for public benefits. It is an entirely different question whether the nation affords the human costs associated with the same policies. One consequence of the generous welfare policies in Norway is deterioration in work ethic. The TV series *Lilyhammer*, starring *Sopranos* actor

Steven Van Zandt as an American expat to Norway, regularly makes fun of the lack of work discipline in the country.

This phenomenon is also apparent outside popular culture. In 2014 the *Financial Times* reported: "Norway's statistics office says many people have started to call Friday *fridag* or "free day" in Norwegian. The state railway company says commuter trains serving the capital are less full on Fridays, and the main toll road operator says traffic is noticeably quieter on Fridays and on Mondays."[22] It is not only the adults who have stopped focusing on work. The youth—born and raised in a system with little reward for work—have gone even further. In a recent survey three out of four Norwegian employers answered that Swedish youth working in the country have a better work ethic than Norwegian youth. Out of those questioned, merely 2 percent believed that young Norwegians between the ages of sixteen and twenty-four have a high work capacity. Stein André Haugerund, president of the employment company Proffice, which conducted the survey, argued that the Norwegian welfare model has created a situation where incentives for hard work are limited, which in turn affects the behavior of youth.[23]

Those who doubt that generous welfare systems can affect working norms should think hard about the case of Norway. It is difficult to disregard the fact that Norwegians just one or two generations ago had among the strongest working ethics in the world. Without high trust, social cohesion, and a culture focused on individual responsibility, Norway would never have grown so successful. The country's oil wealth has boosted the economy further, but has also proved a double-edged sword, since the massive revenues to the state made it possible to fund a very generous welfare system. From a progressive viewpoint, one could, of course, argue that Norway has it all. By relying on oil money, the government can cling to the democratic socialist ideals that its Nordic neighbors have begun to abandon. However, much as in oil-rich Saudi Arabia, handouts have fostered a class of socially poor.

A good example is given in the article "The Confessions of a 'Welfare Freeloader,'" published in the Norwegian daily paper *Dagbladet*. There, a young man named Vegard Skjervheim related that he had been supported by welfare for three years, although he is vital and in his prime. And he was not alone: "I know several people—talented, gifted people—who do not take a job," Skjervheim wrote. They do not do much else either, seen from a societal standpoint. No studies, no clearly defined plan for the future and no cunning plans to create wealth of any kind. The interest to 'participate' or to 'help' is minimal within this group, and poses no motivation to talk about. The feeling of responsibility when it comes to an abstract entity as 'society' is low."[24] The article spurred a national debate about the need to adjust the generosity of the Norwegian welfare state. Even in the oil-rich nation it has become evident that overly generous benefits are creating rather than combating poverty.

An important political question is if there can ever be such a thing as too much welfare. Is it possible that in some circumstances individuals may be better off receiving less generous public support? Gordon B. Dahl, Andreas Ravndal Kostøl, and Magne Mogstad have used an ingenious method to give a conclusive answer. In social sciences, it is often tricky to prove that one thing actually causes the other. The best way to separate causation (A causes B) from correlation (A and B both happen at the same time, without one causing the other) is to use so-called *natural experiments*. Dahl, Kostøl, and Mogstad explain that there is an ongoing debate regarding the link between welfare policy and poverty: "Some policy makers and researchers have argued that a causal relationship exists, creating a culture in which welfare use reinforces itself through the family. Others argue the determinants of poverty or poor health are correlated across generations in ways that have nothing to do with a welfare culture."[25]

These claims are difficult to test scientifically because many factors can explain the link between children's behavior and parents' tendency to rely on welfare. However, the authors found a natural experiment that made it possible to isolate the effect of welfare generosity. In the Norwegian welfare system, judges are sometimes appointed to look at disability insurance claims that have initially been denied. Some appeal judges are systematically more lenient when it comes to granting benefits. From the claimants' perspective, whether the judge appointed is strict or lenient is random; therefore, researchers can compare those who are granted disability insurance by a lenient judge with those who are denied the benefit by a strict judge. The conclusion is clear. The authors found "strong evidence for a causal link across generations: when a parent is allowed [disability insurance] at the appeal stage, their adult child's participation over the next five years increases by 6 percentage points. This effect grows over time, rising to 12 percentage points after 10 years. Although these findings are specific to our setting, they highlight that welfare reforms can have long-lasting effects on program participation, since any original effect on the current generation could be reinforced by changing the participation behavior of their children as well."[26] In other words, overly generous welfare can indeed create a poverty trap for families, producing a social marginalization that is transferred from parent to children. As both Reagan and Roosevelt pointed out, this poverty trap is to be taken seriously.

Overly generous welfare can indeed create a poverty trap

for families.

I myself grew up in a family supported by welfare handouts in Sweden. We moved between various neighborhoods that had one thing in common: many of their residents were immigrant families supported by the government rather than work. Even at a young age I could see that the difficulty for immigrants to find employment, coupled with generous welfare handouts that sometimes made it more lucrative to sit at home rather than work, created social exclusion. Both parents and their children became pacified. This simple observation tells us much about poverty in modern society. In previous generations (and in present-day poor countries) those born in impoverished families were often hungry, had poor or no housing, could not afford education, and even lacked the means to buy the decent clothing they needed for interviews. Today, in most if not all modern societies, underprivileged citizens can rely on various public programs to get their basic needs, such as housing and food, covered. Essential education is free, and scholarships are available to fund higher degrees. The global marketplace has created cheap clothing of good quality. From a distance it is difficult to spot a shirt made by an expensive Italian tailor versus one bought cheaply off the racks of the Gap or H&M. But this does not mean that the obstacles to escape poverty have vanished. Still today, those born poor often remain poor, and in turn pass social marginalization to their children.

Nobel Prize winner Robert Fogel has suggested that poverty exists in modern societies to a large degree because of an uneven distribution of "spiritual resources," such as self-esteem, a sense of discipline, and a sense of community.[27] Poverty is thus not only a material concept, but also a social one. It is clear that basic welfare institutions help alleviate material poverty by redistributing money and services to the less well off. But what role does the welfare state play in social poverty? To some degree welfare states can also alleviate social poverty. For example, in societies where even those born in poor families can access high-quality education, this gives the youth a sense of hope. However, the spiritual poverty that Fogel points to can be made worse when individuals who could otherwise be self-reliant become dependent on public support. When parents become trapped in dependency, their children's behavior and self-esteem also seem to be affected. This is what Ronald Reagan meant when he said that the "most insidious effect of welfare is its usurpation of the role of provider," pointing to how "government programs ruptured the bonds holding poor families together."[28]

So we see that both Roosevelt and Reagan had good reasons to fear how the social fabric and human well-being could inadvertently be negatively affected by welfare dependency. Although Nordic welfare states seemed initially able to avoid this moral hazard, today we know beyond doubt that this was not the case. Even the northern European welfare states—founded in societies with exceptionally strong working ethics and emphasis on individual responsibility—have with time caught up to Roosevelt's harsh predictions. Politicians on both the right and left in this part of the world are therefore seeking to formulate new social contracts, with greater emphasis on incentives for work and personal responsibility. The cradle-to-grave welfare model has lost some of its appeal, and politicians are increasingly turning to market mechanisms. Perhaps American progressives can learn a lesson from all this? After all, the basic idea of welfare policy is to help disadvantaged groups to create a better future for themselves and their families. Evidently overly generous welfare is not always the best way of accomplishing this goal. There is something as too much generosity.

9

WHERE DOES THE AMERICAN DREAM
COME TRUE?

AMERICAN PROGRESSIVES INCREASINGLY ARGUE THAT the "American" Dream is realized, not in America, but in Nordic countries. The *Huffington Post* has, for example, published a piece titled "If You Want the American Dream, Go to Finland." Journalist Blake Fleetwood explains: "Consider what Ed Miliband, the popular British Labor leader—and would-be Prime Minister—said to a conference on social mobility last year: 'If you are born in a more equal society like Finland, Norway, or Denmark, then you have a better chance of moving into a good job than if you are born poor in the United States.' This is a sad, depressing state of affairs for the U.S. and is becoming more true every day."[1] In the *VC Reporter* Raymond Freeman argued that one should "move to 'socialist' Sweden or 'socialist' Denmark" to achieve the American Dream.[2] In the *Los Angeles Times*, Ann Jones wrote, "All the Nordic countries broadly agree that only when people's basic needs are met—when they cease to worry about jobs, education, healthcare, transportation, etc.—can they truly be free to do as they like. While the U.S. settles for the fantasy that every kid has an equal shot at the American dream, Nordic social welfare systems lay the foundations for a more authentic equality and individualism."[3]

Perhaps not surprisingly, politicians on the left in the Nordics support this idea. Norway's former Social Democrat prime minister Jens Stoltenberg similarly claimed in 2013, "The opportunity to achieve the American Dream is larger in Norway than it is in the United States."[4] The same year Danish Social Democrat minister for trade and European affairs Nick Haekkerup declared, "The American dream, if I may be bold, comes to life in Denmark, in a welfare society."[5] Recently Stefan Löfven, the only current Social Democrat prime minister in the Nordics, joined in. Speaking at an elderly care home he said, "In the United States they often talk about the American Dream. But for many it remains just that—a dream which is never realized. In Sweden we use [social] tools to make sure that the dream turns into reality."[6]

It is interesting to examine this argument in greater detail. In 1931 historian James Truslow Adams coined the term *American Dream* in his book *The Epic of America*. According to Adams, the dream was of a "social order in which each man and each woman shall be able to attain the fullest stature of which they are innately capable."[7] Today many, particularly on the left, challenge the idea that the American Dream actually can be realized in America. Rather, they believe that the dream comes true through social democracy. In 2004 Jeremy Rifkin published the book *The European Dream: How Europe's Vision of the Future Is Quickly Eclipsing the American Dream*. There he explained that the American Dream captures the hopes of immigrants who left Europe to seek opportunities in the United States a hundred years ago. Today, however, according to Rifkin, this dream has turned into a nightmare: "the great American myth of upward mobility continues to live on, despite mounting evidence that what was once a great dream has become, for many, a relentless nightmare." Instead it is the Old World in Europe that, through large welfare states, is "slowly becoming the new land of opportunity."[8]

It certainly sounds dramatic that the American Dream has turned into some sort of nightmarish scenario. Surely if not America but rather European welfare states are making this dream come true, this proves that the American social model has lost its soul. Perhaps it is time to adopt a European-style welfare state in the United States? Those who make this argument can find some support in research. To be more precise, a number of studies compare the incomes of parents with those of their children. These studies tend to find that the link between the prosperity of parents and children is higher in the United States than in Nordic countries. This means that children in the Nordics move to an income class different from their parents' more often than children in the United States do.[9] This is interpreted as proof that the opportunities for upward mobility are more limited in American society.

The idea that the Nordic systems offer greater social mobility is understandingly gaining attention among welfare state proponents. It is also a striking argument for those who wish to criticize American capitalism. The reason is, of course, that America long has been viewed as the land of opportunity. But what if America isn't the land of opportunity? What if

Nordic social democracy creates better opportunities for class mobility? Some far-reaching conclusions have been based on the observation that parental incomes have a stronger link to the incomes of their children in the United States than in the Nordics. Markus Jäntti and his fellow researchers, for example, claim that this shows that the idea of American exceptionalism, coined originally by Alexis de Tocqueville to describe high rates of social mobility in the United States, "may need to be viewed in a new light."[10] But all these conclusions are, ultimately, based on comparing apples with oranges.

The simple fact is that Nordic societies are much more homogenous than the American melting pot. Until recently, when immigrants started flowing into the Nordics, the vast majority of the populations in these countries had the same culture. And that culture was a Nordic one, with great emphasis on hard work, individual responsibility, social cohesion, and trust. Of course, the stronger link between the outcome of parents and their children in the United States is because the country is considerably more diverse. Much of the income difference exists because different groups, such as Asians, whites, and African-Americans, have different average incomes. Indeed, studies do find that more than half of the link between parental incomes and that of the children in the United States is due to persistence of earnings differences across racial and ethnic groups.[11]

When you think about it, it simply doesn't make sense to compare the highly diverse American society with highly homogenous Nordic societies. A better analogy would be to compare the Nordic countries with a small part of the United States, populated mainly by a single ethic group. How strong is, for example, social mobility within the parts of Utah populated mainly by the Mormons, compared to within Denmark? How strong is it among the parts of Minnesota populated largely by those of Nordic descent, compared to within Sweden? Unfortunately, as far as I know, researchers haven't gathered the data necessary for carrying out this analysis. But there is a way of comparing apples with apples so we can figure out if it is the American or the Nordic model that offers the greatest opportunities for upward mobility: look at immigrants. The American Dream is ultimately about the chances that society grants to recent immigrants. Immigrants are an interesting group since they are part of the minority population both in the Nordic countries and in America. By looking at the opportunities of those born abroad, it becomes possible to figure out where the American Dream really comes to life for people who start with an empty hand. So let's begin the comparison.

> By looking at the opportunities of those born abroad, it becomes possible to figure out where the American Dream really comes to life for people who start with an empty hand.

One of the best indicators of integration is the possibility to get a job. As the following table shows, the United States is far ahead of the Nordic countries in this regard. In America those who are born abroad actually have a higher employment rate than the native born, while in the Nordics they have much lower rates. This might come as a surprise to those who believe that

Nordic societies have created a system where just about anybody can succeed. It is, however, common knowledge for those who follow the development in northern Europe. Studies show that European welfare states are quite bad when it comes to giving immigrants the opportunity to find jobs. The Nordic countries are particularly bad at this, which comes as no surprise since they have extensive welfare systems. The United States, on the other hand, having a smaller government model, is quite good at integrating the foreign born in the labor market.[12] This, of course, makes sense. In countries where the government taxes you heavily when you work and gives you generous benefits when you don't, the incentives to finding a job are more limited. Taxes also reduce entrepreneurship and growth of existing businesses, which reduces the creation of new jobs. Lastly, welfare states tend to have rigid labor market laws, which also reduce job growth. Since immigrants are outsiders in the job market, they are particularly sensitive to the effects of high taxes, generous welfare benefits, and strict labor laws.

EMPLOYMENT LEVELS COMPARING NATIVE BORN TO FOREIGN BORN

COUNTRY	FOREIGN BORN HAS
UNITED STATES	4% HIGHER EMPLOYMENT RATE THAN NATIVE BORN
FINLAND	6% LOWER EMPLOYMENT RATE THAN NATIVE BORN
NORWAY	10% LOWER EMPLOYMENT RATE THAN NATIVE BORN
DENMARK	11% LOWER EMPLOYMENT RATE THAN NATIVE BORN
SWEDEN	15% LOWER EMPLOYMENT RATE THAN NATIVE BORN

Source: OECD and author's calculations.

The employment rate among those born in Somalia is merely 21 percent in Sweden, far less than the 54 percent in the United States.

Of course, looking at immigrants as a single group doesn't really tell us enough. Some immigrants have university degrees while others only have basic education, or in extreme cases are illiterate. So let's separate skilled immigrants from less skilled ones. We certainly know that low-skilled immigrants face great difficulties in creating a future for themselves in Nordic countries. One example is Somali immigrants. A Swedish government report has shown that the employment rate among those born in Somalia is merely 21 percent in Sweden, far less than the 54 percent in the United States.[13] Similarly, in Denmark and Norway half of those born in Somalia are neither employed nor educated.[14] The point isn't that Somali immigrants are thriving in the United States. They still have limited education, low incomes, and high unemployment, but over half of the Somalis in the United States do have a job. This is far from the case in Sweden, where only one-fifth do. Once we compare apples to apples, the case for the American Dream coming true in the Nordics rather than America isn't looking that compelling.

Now, let's compare immigrants with a low education level with native-born individuals who are similarly educated. As the following table shows, the relative employment prospects of the immigrants are much better in the American labor market. In the United States immigrants with a low education level have considerably lower unemployment than native Americans with similar educational level. In all Nordic countries, the immigrants have a higher unemployment level. What does this tell us? One explanation is, of course, that the Nordic welfare state model is making it more difficult to find work. The Nordic countries follow the same economic laws as the rest of the world. Generous public handouts, strict regulations on the job market, and high taxes do affect employment opportunities for outsiders. Another way of looking at it is that the native born in the Nordics are prospering due to the unique Nordic success norms. Since it is culture, rather than the welfare state, that explains much of the success of the region, we shouldn't be surprised that the success of the natives isn't transferred to those born abroad.

UNEMPLOYMENT LEVELS BETWEEN LOW-EDUCATED NATIVE BORN AND FOREIGN BORN

COUNTRY	LOW-EDUCATED FOREIGN BORN UNEMPLOYMENT IS
UNITED STATES	4% **LOWER** THAN LOW-EDUCATED NATIVE BORN
DENMARK	6% HIGHER THAN LOW-EDUCATED NATIVE BORN
NORWAY	7% HIGHER THAN LOW-EDUCATED NATIVE BORN
FINLAND	9% HIGHER THAN LOW-EDUCATED NATIVE BORN
SWEDEN	10% HIGHER THAN LOW-EDUCATED NATIVE BORN

Source: OECD and author's calculations.

So what about immigrants who have studied for a higher degree? The odd thing about the Nordics is that even skilled immigrants struggle to get a job. A paper by Kristian Rose Tronstad at the Institute for Labor and Social Research in Norway shows that the poor integration of Somali immigrants in the Norwegian labor market could in part be explained by factors such as low education and lack of social capital. Tronstad reported that labor market exclusion is also true for Iranian migrants in the country. This is more surprising, since "Iranians are mainly political refugees with rather long duration of residence in Norway. They are mostly from urban areas; as secular as most Norwegian, educational level is relatively high for both men and women."[15] A study by Statistics Norway confirms this. The study finds that Iranians in Norway have unusually high educational levels when compared to other immigrant groups. Still, the group had almost as high unemployment rates as those born in Somalia. At the time of the study, fully 41 percent of adult Iranians surveyed responded that they were unemployed and actively seeking work at some point during the latest year. This is only slightly lower than the rate among those born in Somalia, where 44 percent were unemployed and seeking work.[16]

In Sweden, it is difficult to find studies where the outcomes for groups born in different parts of the world are shown separately. Some studies, however, report historic data for specific minority views. One such study follows the prospects of Iranian immigrants, who, as in Norway, are a highly educated group. In 1999, some fifteen years after the average Iranian had migrated to Sweden, a large segment was still trapped in welfare dependency. Fully a third of Iranian households were at the time supported by welfare handouts. Another third were mainly supported by various forms of public transfers, with some additional work income. Merely a third of Iranian households supported themselves mainly through work, almost exclusively through low-income jobs.[17]

Another Swedish study has calculated the incomes of immigrants to Sweden from Iran and Turkey. Between 1993 and 2000, the income from work for the average Iranian immigrant was only 61 percent of the average income of a native Swede. For Turkish immigrants the corresponding figure was 74 percent.[18] We can compare this to American data for roughly the same period. According to the U.S. Census for 2000, those born in Iran had an income that was 136 percent of the average for native-born residents, compared to 114 percent for those born in Turkey.[19] Granted, the individuals who migrated from Turkey and Iran to the United States were not identical to those who went to Sweden. But many of them did have similar backgrounds. Most of those who traveled to Sweden and the United States belonged to Turkey's and Iran's middle classes. It seems that while many achieved the American Dream in the United States, few did so in Sweden.

Some Iranians who migrated to America belonged to the upper class, bringing wealth with them. A better comparison is immigrants to Canada, who, like those to Sweden, mainly came from the middle class.[20] Data from Statistics Canada shows that the majority of the Iranian population living in the country in 2006 had come during the last five years. Their full-time work income was on average C$47,000 annually. This is just slightly below the Canadian average of C$51,000. The unemployment among Iranians was 10 percent, only somewhat above the average of 7 percent in the country.[21] The Canadian system, with a free labor market and greater incentives to work, obviously granted more chances for work to the Iranians than the Swedish system.

[In Sweden] outsiders are not nearly as successful, as even

the highly educated immigrants struggle to find work.

Another example is a group of well-educated Iraqi citizens who fled from Saddam Hussein's reign to Sweden at the end of the 1980s and the beginning of the 1990s. Those Iraqis who arrived and stayed in Sweden between 1987 and 1991 were almost all highly educated. The group was 2.3 times as likely to have a higher education of more than three years compared to native Swedes. However, even this elite group struggled to find work in the Swedish labor market. In 1995, only 13 percent of the women and 23 percent of the men were employed.[22] There really can't be any doubt about this: while Sweden on paper looks like a country that offers people the chance to climb the social ladder, an important reason for this is that most Swedes have the same cultural background. Outsiders are not nearly as successful, as even the highly educated immigrants struggle to find work.

Of course, one reason for the differences is that different groups of immigrants are attracted to different countries. Economics professors Assaf Razin and Jackline Wahba explain that there is "growing literature on how welfare-state generosity works as a magnet to migrants." The reason is that individuals who have valuable skills prefer to live in countries with low taxes, where they can keep the fruit of their work. Those who have less-valuable skills are attracted to countries where generous welfare systems provide them with tax-funded benefits.[23] Not surprisingly, the research literature shows that highly qualified labor migrants tend to migrate to countries where wages for experts are high and taxes are low.[24] This is a partial explanation for the difficulties that the Nordic countries are facing when it comes to integrating foreign-born people: to a large degree, their social systems are attracting those with low skill sets, while the more skilled migrants are going to America and other low-tax countries. However, as the example of the highly educated Iranian and Iraqi immigrants shows, selection is just part of the problem: the Nordic welfare states fail to integrate even the highly skilled migrants. We can look at how highly educated immigrants on average fare in different countries. As shown in the following table, America again comes at top. While highly educated immigrants in the United States have marginally higher unemployment rates than natives with similar educational background, the gaps are considerably higher in the Nordic countries.

THE DIFFERENCE IN UNEMPLOYMENT BETWEEN HIGH-EDUCATED NATIVE BORN AND FOREIGN BORN

COUNTRY	HIGH-EDUCATED FOREIGN BORN UNEMPLOYMENT IS
UNITED STATES	1% HIGHER UNEMPLOYMENT THAN HIGH-EDUCATED NATIVE BORN
NORWAY	3% HIGHER UNEMPLOYMENT THAN LOW EDUCATED NATIVE BORN
DENMARK	5% HIGHER UNEMPLOYMENT THAN LOW-EDUCATED NATIVE BORN
SWEDEN	8% HIGHER UNEMPLOYMENT THAN LOW-EDUCATED NATIVE BORN
FINLAND	8% HIGHER UNEMPLOYMENT THAN LOW-EDUCATED NATIVE BORN

Source: OECD and author's calculations.

Could the reason be discrimination? A way of explaining why immigrants have a greater chance of getting a job in the United States is that American society is more inclusive culturally, while Nordic societies are exclusive. There is indeed a case to be made for the Nordic countries combining a cold climate with a rather cold culture. Scandinavian culture isn't outgoing; therefore, immigrants often find it difficult to make new friends. In American society, immigrants can more easily bond with their neighbors and by doing so, gain a foothold in society. After comedian Gregory Poehler (brother of *Saturday Night Live* star Amy Poehler) moved to Sweden with his girlfriend, he decided to star in a comedy show about his real-life experiences with culture shock as an American moving to Sweden. The show, *Welcome to Sweden*, regularly makes fun of Swedish habits of social isolation. For example, some Swedes look through the peephole of their apartment doors before they go out: they want to make sure they won't run into neighbors when they are leaving, since having to greet the neighbors is seen as a social inconvenience.

Many immigrants view the Swedes, and other Nordic people, as hostile since they seldom have a relation to their neighbors. What the immigrants sometimes fail to realize is that this isn't necessarily racism, but rather, simply part of Scandinavian culture. The World Value Survey has measured how common racist views are. The survey includes only Sweden out of the Nordic countries. It turns out that less than 4 percent of Swedes would mind having foreign-born neighbors, as compared to 14 percent in the United States. Similarly, 14 percent of Swedes believe that employers should give priority to natives, compared with 50 percent of Americans.[25] So, although foreigners in Sweden can struggle to get acquainted with their neighbors, outright discrimination is quite uncommon in the country.

According to Swedish economist Andreas Bergh, the explanation for why Nordic countries fail in integration is simple: welfare state policies and labor union wage setting. Through a statistical analysis he found that two factors significantly influence job prospects for immigrants: "First, welfare state generosity keeps immigrants away from the labor force. Second, given that immigrants enter the labor force, collective bargaining agreements explain immigrant unemployment."[26] The Nordic system, where labor unions negotiate nearly all wages in medium-sized and large places of employment, gives strong influence for worker's organizations. But these organizations represent the interest of those who have a job, not necessarily those who are outside the job market. Unions push for high entry-level jobs in collective bargaining. These high entry-level wages make it difficult for immigrants (and the youth) to enter the job market.

Indeed, the generous welfare systems of the Nordic countries do not only provide various forms of social good. They can also directly counteract the American Dream by creating dependency and hindering buildup of social and financial capital through work. In the paper "Immigration as a Challenge to the Danish Welfare State?" Peter Nannestad explains how welfare state benefits can reduce incentives to work as well as acquire new skills:

> In addition to broad coverage, transfer payments in the Danish welfare state are also quite generous relative to minimum wages in the labor market. Thus the welfare state weakens economic incentives for labor market participation, especially for lowskilled, low-paid

individuals. While the net present value of social benefits may be a little lower than the net present value of earnings from labor even for unskilled immigrant workers in Denmark, the difference to the net present value of earnings in their homelands will normally still be large. Due to their relatively low educational achievement levels, this applies to a rather large proportion of the population of immigrants and descendants from non-western countries in Denmark. Through the same mechanism the welfare state may also weaken immigrants' incentives to invest in acquiring the necessary preconditions for labor marked participation, like minimum levels of language and social skills.[27]

A paper published by the OECD shines light on the same problem. There we can read about the concept of the "benefit trap":

One factor that discourages immigrants from working is the low economic return, compared with living on public income support. The Danish welfare system is generous: so-called "short-term" benefits such as unemployment insurance and social assistance are intended to provide people back to supporting themselves . . . For native Danes, the system appears to fulfil this role, in sharp contrast to the situation of migrants . . . Migrants from non-western countries are particularly vulnerable to finding themselves in a welfare trap because their average earnings prospects are so much lower than for native Danes. Seen in that light, it is remarkable that around one in five immigrants and descendants in work would be financially better off drawing unemployment insurance, while another third gain less than [Danish kronas] 500 per month by working . . . The situation for these low paid workers does not show any improvement until they have been working around five years.[28]

Again, we see that serious research goes against the Shangri-La view of the Nordics as a part of the world where the normal laws of the economic universe don't work. Of course one could argue in favor of systems with generous welfare or strong labor unions. But such policies come with a high cost: if entry-level wages are set at a high level and government benefits are almost as generous as work income for some workers, unemployment will rise. The Nordic lesson is simply that immigration, particularly of groups with limited skills, is quite difficult to combine with generous welfare policy and high entry-level wages.

> The Nordic lesson is simply that immigration, particularly of groups with limited skills, is quite difficult to combine with generous welfare policy and high entry-level wages.

Could wealthy Norway, which has the oil wealth to pay for a more generous system than in the other Nordic countries, provide good opportunities for immigrants to prosper? After all, the oil wealth boosts demand for labor. Kristian Rose Tronstad explains that this high demand is offset by the fact that centralized union wage bargaining creates "barriers for less productive jobseekers, as offering their labor to lower price is not an option." In addition: "[s]trict employment protection legislation implies that both the hiring and firing are costly, and employers therefore are reluctant to take risk."[29] Again we see that welfare state institutions are hindering the American Dream. It is worth mentioning that the differences in unemployment between natives and foreign-born people in the Nordics, as this chapter has shown, are likely underestimated. Official statistics in the Nordic welfare states hide the true unemployment rates within the welfare systems.

In Norway, this practice is quite evident. In particular, early retirement through disability pension is routinely used to classify long-term unemployed individuals who are healthy enough to work as being outside of the labor force. One study looked at individuals ages thirty to fifty-five who were granted disability pension between 1992 and 2003. This group includes 11 percent of the men and 16 percent of the women with Norwegian background. Of course, it makes little sense that a healthy country such as Norway would have a large share of its middle-aged population being actually disabled. Rather, many of those classified as disabled are simply unemployed. The trick of hiding unemployment in early retirement is even more routinely used to lower the official unemployment rate of immigrants. The same study found that a quarter of those in the same age group and born in the Middle East and North Africa in Norway were given disability pension during the same period.[30]

Of course, having a job isn't the only thing that matters. The Nordic welfare states are famous for their good social and health performance. The citizens of these countries, including immigrants, enjoy universal access to health care, day care for children, elderly care, schooling, and higher education. Although the generous welfare states hinder the ability of immigrants to land a job, it is quite conceivable that these universal systems would be able to transfer favorable health outcomes to immigrants. How does the American system compare with the Nordic ones in this regard?

It is a bit tricky to compare health outcomes between different societies. One way is by looking at the Better Policies for Better Lives project, an international benchmarking that gathers information on life quality around the world. This project measures the share of foreign-born adults who themselves report to be in good health. Surprisingly, the United States has better outcomes than all Nordic countries in this regard. A much larger share of immigrants in the United States report that they are of good health. How can we understand this difference? Is it, at least in part, because different groups of foreign-born people are attracted to the United States? Or because definitions of good health differ? The significant difference in favor of the United States at the very least supports the idea that good health outcomes in the Nordics relate to the healthy cultures that people in this part of the world have. Evidently, this is not simply transmitted to those who have arrived from other parts of the world. Indeed, in the Nordic countries themselves it is widely acknowledged that

SHARE OF IMMIGRANTS WHO IDENTIFY THEMSELVES AS NOT IN GOOD HEALTH

COUNTRY	IMMIGRANTS NOT IN GOOD HEALTH
UNITED STATES	12%
FINLAND	19%
NORWAY	28%
SWEDEN	29%
DENMARK	32%

Source: OECD Better Policies for Better Lives.[31]

significant gaps exist in health outcomes between the native born and immigrants.[32] The myth of the nearly perfect Nordic health sector is more commonly found abroad.

Another relevant social factor is educational results. Foreign-born adults face greater obstacles in the Nordic labor markets compared to in the American one. However, it is possible that the children of immigrants would succeed in the Nordics by taking advantage of the publicly funded school systems in these countries. After all, the entire education system—from kindergarten to high school, university, and doctorate-level studies—is funded by the government in the Nordics. Surely this can create opportunities for upward mobility. The PISA (Program for International Student Assessment) global survey, often cited when comparing different school systems, measures the outcomes of children born of immigrant parents. Here, Finland, which is famous for its well-functioning school system, is ahead of the United States. However, the educational outcomes of the children of immigrants is better in the United States than in the other three Nordic countries.[33]

PISA SCORES OF THE CHILDREN OF IMMIGRANTS

COUNTRY	PISA SCORE
FINLAND	493
UNITED STATES	484
NORWAY	463
SWEDEN	454
DENMARK	446

Source: OECD Better Policies for Better Lives. The average PISA score in developed countries for all students is 500.

Studies from the Nordic countries have highlighted the challenges faced by children who themselves are immigrants, or who are native-born children of parents who have come as immigrants.[34] One explanation is that the lack of opportunities for the parents to go from welfare dependency to work creates social poverty, which in turn affects the future opportunities of the children.[35] The marginalized situation created by welfare traps in the Nordic systems can thus affect intergenerational mobility over the generations, also in school performance. Again we see that the American Dream of upward mobility, once we compare apples to apples by looking at immigrants, simply seems to be in favor of America rather than the Nordics. The American Dream continues to be more alive in the country after which it is named.

The American Dream continues to be more alive in the country after which it is named.

Those who criticize the lack of upward mobility in America do have an important point. We should be worried about the fact that many who are born in poor families remain there. The fight against inequality in the United States should be given high priority. In this regard, perhaps some lessons can be learned from the Nordic approach. For example, of course life chances are evened out by an education system where students are not inhibited by lack of parental income from going to college. However, as this chapter has shown, the welfare states make it difficult for outsiders to become self-sufficient. The social success for which the Nordic countries are famous is mainly limited to those who have Nordic cultural origins. This tells us that introducing a Nordic-style democratic socialism in the United States is not the way of making the American Dream come true. More taxes, more benefits, greater labor union control, and more labor legislation are likely to instead shut the door to upward mobility.

10

SWEDEN'S SELF-INFLICTED

IMMIGRATION CRISIS

IF YOU FOLLOW AMERICAN MEDIA, perhaps you already know that Sweden is experiencing something of an immigration crisis. Toward the end of 2015, Benjamin Teitelbaum wrote an op-ed piece in the *New York Times*. For a newspaper that usually has a pro-immigration stand, the title of the article was quite astonishing: "Sweden's Self-Inflicted Nightmare." Teitelbaum explained why Sweden's open immigration policies had turned into a quite unmanageable situation:

> Sweden, a country of 9.6 million, lately has been absorbing 10,000 asylum seekers per week, and expects the total number coming into the country this year alone to reach 190,000—a population greater than that of its fourth largest city. Since the intensification of the immigration crisis in September, municipalities have complained that they lack housing, teachers and classroom space, and doctors for the newcomers. The police have acknowledged that they've lost

the ability to monitor the whereabouts of foreign nationals within the country. Migration agencies have signaled that they can no longer ensure that unaccompanied minors passing through their offices will be transferred into acceptable living conditions. And leaked emails have shown that government officials are panicking over how they will pay for associated costs.[1]

Similarly, the *Washington Post* published an article titled "Even Europe's Humanitarian Superpower Is Turning Its Back on Refugees." Authors Griff Witte and Anthony Faiola explained:

> When the small, crumpled body of 3-year-old Alan Kurdi washed up on the Aegean coast Sept. 2, Europe's humanitarian super-power sprang into action. Sweden's prime minister headlined gala fundraisers, Swedish celebrities starred in telethons, and a country that prides itself on doing the right thing seemed to rally as one to embrace refugees fleeing for their lives. But after taking in more asylum seekers per capita than any other nation in Europe, Sweden's welcome mat now lies in tatters. Overwhelmed by the human tide of 2015, the center-left government is deploying extraordinary new border controls and slashing benefits in an unmistakable signal to refugees contemplating the long trek to Sweden in the new year: Stay out.[2]

To understand what is happening in Sweden, we must turn to 2010, when the country took a turn toward free immigration. That year, a center-right government led by Sweden's then moderate prime minister Fredrik Reinfeldt was reelected. However, during the election the anti-immigration Sweden

Democrats gained enough votes to enter the Parliament. The government reacted by signing a deal with the opposition environmental party, which in effect opened up Sweden for nearly free immigration. Later, Reinfeldt explained that his ambition was to isolate Sweden Democrats from power by turning politics in the opposite direction following their rise to power.

> Being against open borders [had] became synonymous with being a racist.

Some intellectuals warned that free immigration might not be the best idea. Although reasonable enough, the warnings did not prove popular. Progressive ideas about immigration came to dominate the debate in Sweden, and anybody who voiced criticism toward free immigration was branded as being narrow minded. Being against open borders became synonymous with being a racist. The prevailing attitude was that Sweden would benefit from large rates of inflows. My brother, Tino Sanandaji, was one of the few who voiced criticism against this idea. He was often alone in using facts and figures to argue that the idealistic view that open borders would benefit society was simply not true. To understand the Swedish immigration crisis, one must bear in mind a number of facts, which can seem quite astonishing for an international audience, and were seldom acknowledged during the years when favoring open borders was the only legitimate political view in the country.

First, the Swedish welfare state is very bad at integrating

foreigners into its job market. In chapter 9 we saw that immigrants struggle to enter the job markets of Sweden and other Nordic countries. Generous welfare benefits, high taxes, and rigid labor market regulations are simply holding immigrants back. During later years Swedish politics has taken a sharp turn toward less extensive welfare policies. Taxes have been cut, welfare benefits reduced, and labor legislation relaxed. These changes, often called job-fare policies, have boosted job creation in Sweden. Amongst the Swedish right, the conviction grew that job-fare had made it possible to remove borders and open the country for foreign influx. But this is simply not the case. Sweden is a knowledge-intensive economy where higher education is often needed to find employment. Many simple jobs have been automated. Factories have invested in robots, and many stores are moving toward self-checkouts. Immigrants who don't know Swedish and have limited education simply don't fit in. Even after the job-fare reforms, many find themselves in a situation where welfare checks are as rewarding as pay slips.

Dagens Nyheter is a leading daily newspaper in Sweden, which is strongly pro-immigrant. However, even *Dagens Nyheter* at times acknowledges the massive difficulties that the Swedish welfare states have when it comes to integration. Through an in-depth study, the newspaper has followed the outcomes of all refugees granted asylum in Sweden in 2004. Journalists at *Dagens Nyheter* ask a simple question: how had the future shaped out for them ten years later? The reality was grim to say the least. The median income of the refugees was merely 11,100 Swedish kronor ($1,300) a month, much lower than the Swedish average of 23,700 kronor ($2,800). The family immigrants of refugees earned even less. Ten years after arriving in the country, their median income was as low as 4,500 kronor a month ($530). These very low incomes show that a large segment of all refugees, and likely the vast majority of family immigrants, were not working and instead relying on welfare support. *Dagens Nyheter* found that at least four out of ten refugees ten years after arrival were still supported by welfare. The newspaper acknowledged that this is likely a significant underestimation, since some municipalities refused to give the journalists the paperwork needed to match individuals to welfare receipts.[3]

That many immigrants are trapped in welfare dependency, or have low incomes, is a major concern in Sweden. The reason is simple: the country has a generous welfare state, a system that only works if the majority of the population have jobs through which large contributions are made to the tax agency. Perhaps more important, immigration has brought on major social upheaval to Sweden. Remember our quote in chapter 1 from *Time* magazine in 1976, which described Sweden as a "materialist paradise," where "no slumps disfigure [the] cities"?[4] Well, this isn't the case anymore. It is certainly true that those parts of a city that have an overwhelming Swedish population are typically far from slums. But areas where many immigrants live are a different story altogether.

The Liberal Party in Sweden, which is part of the center-right alliance, used to track the number of socially marginalized city parts in the country.[5] The definition is simple: less than 60 percent of adults are employed and the city part either has low participation in the democratic process (less than 70 percent had voted in the latest local election) or low school results (share of students who pass ninth grade is under 70 percent). In countries such as the United States, many neighborhoods, particularly those populated by poor minorities, fit this description. In 1990, only three city parts in Sweden did. The country really seemed to be a social democratic paradise. But as this book has shown in detail, the reason was that Sweden at the time was a homogenous country where people followed a uniquely successful culture. As immigrants came to Sweden, many of them failed to reach the same social success. In 2002 the number of marginalized city parts had mushroomed to 128. It is worth remembering that this was before the Swedish welfare state had been reduced in size. In 2004 the number had grown to 155, and in 2006, when the center-right parties took over power, there were 156 marginalized city parts.[6]

When the Liberal Party became part of the government, they suddenly stopped reporting about how marginalized city districts in Sweden had developed. The party argued that the workfare policies, which were aimed at reducing dependency on welfare handouts, had successfully combated poverty. Arguably, the policies were successful. But as immigration continued, the number of marginalized neighborhoods continued to grow. In 2014 Tino Sanandaji updated the figures that the Liberal Party themselves previously used, and published an updated version for the think tank the New Welfare Foundation. In panic, the Liberal Party released their own updated version just one day after Tino's report. The results were clear: for the latest available year, 2012, the number of socially marginalized city parts had grown even further, to 186.[7]

The rapid deterioration of immigrant neighborhoods is visible for all to see, and is quite astonishing. In early 2016 Swedish government television reported that the police in Sweden's capital, Stockholm, were on their knees because young men who had migrated from the streets of Morocco and other North African countries were causing massive crime. According to the police, they frequently steal items, abuse security guards, and sexually assault women. When arrested, the young criminals are often released shortly thereafter because authorities lack information about their age, and most of the young men tell the police that they are underage. One police officer explained: "I would never let my children off at Central Station; no police would do that."[8] A recent change is that police carrying automatic weapons are patrolling Stockholm's metro system, to prevent crime as well as the risk of Islamic terrorism.

Criminal shootouts, previously quite uncommon in peaceful Sweden, have become commonplace not only in Stockholm, but also in Sweden's second-largest city, Gothenburg. It is no exaggeration to say that criminal gangs, often of immigrant origin, have wrested control of some parts of Gothenburg from the police. Together the two cities have a combined urban population of around 1.5 million. The capitals of Denmark, Norway, and Finland have a combined population of 3.3 million people, yet between 2010 and the first half of 2015, 298 people were wounded from shootouts in Stockholm and Gothenburg, compared to merely 70 in the three other Nordic capitals combined. So, in effect, the two Swedish cities had almost ten times as high gun wound rates as the other large Nordic cities.[9] Denmark, Norway, and Finland have less of an issue with crime among immigrants simply because they have accepted fewer immigrants. Iceland has barely seen any immigration.

That parts of Swedish cities are turning into something that almost resembles Detroit is a new phenomenon with which the countries' lax law enforcement struggles to cope. In the third-largest city, Malmö, the majority of the population has immigrant background. There the situation is, in many ways, even worse. Recently, criminal gangs have begun using grenades as weapons in the city. Middle-class families have moved away from parts of Malmö, to distance themselves from crime and violence. Even in the smaller Swedish cities there are immigrant neighborhoods in which violence and shootings have become commonplace. Often these crimes are carried out by young men who either themselves have migrated to Sweden, or are the descendants of immigrants.

In February 2016 the Australian edition of *60 Minutes* sent a crew to film a segment on the European refugee crisis in a suburb of Stockholm. The *Washington Times* reported that the crew was protected by six police officers. When the police escort left, the crew was attacked by locals.[10] These kinds of attacks are unfortunately not uncommon. Public servants, bus drivers, and journalists have numerously been targeted by gangs in immigrant neighborhoods. Sometimes police and ambulance staff have been lured by alarms and ambushed by violent gangs.

Welfare policies do not make the country immune to high rates of social exclusion and crime among immigrants.

A part of the explanation might be that Sweden has lax criminal laws and gives too little resources and power to the policy. More important, what we are seeing is a normalization of Sweden compared to the rest of the world. Foreign admirers of Nordic-style social democracy often believe that Nordic policies somehow have eliminated crime. The reality is that Nordic culture has. People who lack the unusual ethics related to individual responsibility, social cohesion, and abiding by the rules that predominated Swedish culture are more likely to turn out on the wrong side of the law. The issue is made worse by the fact that the welfare model makes it difficult for immigrants to get a job, trapping many in a welfare dependency that creates hopelessness. Of course, a question that begs answering is: if Swedish welfare policies do not make the country immune to high rates of social exclusion and crime among immigrants, why should the same policies be expected to solve the social problems of America?

Previously, Sweden had a regulated migration. During the 1990s and the early 2000s the country received around 100 immigrants a week. This is a fairly high number for a small country with a population fewer than 10 million, situated in the cold Nordics, far from the countries from which immigrants come. The brutal civil war in Syria increased migration across Europe, and a growing realization among refugees that Sweden is the most welcoming country for them on the continent combined to increase the inflow substantially. By the end of 2015, around 10,000 immigrants were coming into the country each week.

The Swedish population has shown great openness to this wave of immigrants. Many have volunteered to welcome them and help them reside in the country; many more have donated clothing and other necessities. Almost all municipalities in the country have accepted migrants. However, even meeting the basic needs of refugees soon proved a major constraint on the Swedish welfare system. A survey from late 2015 found that 40 percent of municipalities feel that immigration is putting severe pressure on social services and schools in the short term; 74 percent of municipalities believe that the pressure will also be severe in the long term.[11] In southern Sweden, the refugee influx was so high that all available mattresses were reportedly sold out.[12] Tents have been set up in the freezing Swedish winter to accommodate immigrants.

No one really knows how Sweden, where restrictions on building permits have created a major housing crisis, will deal with the massive immigration inflows. What is apparent is that many immigrant families are sharing the same small apartments. In some neighborhoods overcrowding seems to have reached Third World levels. Adding to all this is that Sweden has also seen immigration of thousands of beggars from Eastern Europe. In nearly all, if not all, Swedish cities, beggars are easy to spot on the streets. Since they are not given (much) welfare support, the beggars have created a number of shantytowns across the country. Shantytowns, grenades thrown in the streets, slums, and rampant gangs is hardly what you would traditionally associate with Sweden. Yet there can be little doubt that these are very real social concerns in today's Sweden, largely as a result of the recent immigration inflows.

The majority of the immigrants are not actually coming from Syria, but from other parts of the world. Sweden accepts most children who come unaccompanied by adults. Contrary to its Nordic neighbors, which are reluctant to accept a large influx of migrants, Swedish authorities have typically accepted the age given by the migrants themselves. Therefore, many Afghan families (many of them living in Iran) have sold their belongings, or borrowed money, to send their oldest child to Sweden in hopes that once one child has been granted asylum, the rest can then follow as family migrants. This make sense, since even if nobody in the family were to find work, the welfare support provided in Sweden creates a much higher standard of living than that to which Afghan families are typically accustomed. The newly arrived are almost exclusively men, and often seem to be much older than actually claimed. As an extreme example, local media reports that a man from Afghanistan accused of raping a child was not fifteen, as he reported, but rather, as evident in his own Facebook profile, forty-five.[13]

On top of this, Sweden offers a special form of government benefit to children who have lost their parents. An administrative court has decided that this benefit should be given to all refugee children who claim to have lost one or both parents, if only they promise to be telling the truth. The benefit can also be given retroactively for the past two years. Thus, a refugee child who simply claims to have lost both of his parents can be given around 70,000 Swedish kronor (close to $9,000) in retroactive support and an additional 35,000 kronor (close to $4,500) each year until he turns eighteen. This may not seem like a huge sum for an American or a Swede, but it is a small fortune in a country such as Afghanistan. As knowledge of this benefit is spreading, an increasing number of refugee children are claiming it. In 2015 around ten thousand children in Sweden, including those born in the country, received government support for having lost their parents. By 2019 this is expected to have mushroomed to thirty thousand children.[14]

These sums are, of course, only a drop in the ocean compared to the total money spent by the Swedish welfare state, but they do illustrate the difficulty of combining extremely progressive ideals with open borders. They also show that immigrants are given huge economic incentives for claiming various government benefits. What do you think happens when a Nordic-style labor market, where high taxes and high entry-level wages make it difficult for immigrants to get a job, is combined with extremely generous benefits? Should we be surprised that many are trapped in dependency and that some even start cheating the system? Is it the immigrants that are to blame or the ill-designed system?

Much of the news relating to immigration and integration in Sweden sounds quite absurd, since the situation is rather unusual. The Swedish system is experiencing a crash from which it is trying to recover. The government that came to power in 2014, a coalition between the Social Democrats and the Environmental Party, were initially nearly paralyzed by the situation. At first, the government expressed support for open borders. In mid-2015 Social Democrat prime minister Stefan Löfven explained that there was "no limit" on the number of refugees that the country could take in.[15] As frustration grew, the Social Democrats fell in the polls, and the anti-immigration Sweden Democrats surged ahead, Löfven suddenly reversed policies. Or, as a headline in the UK's left-leaning *Guardian* read, "Sweden slams shut its open-door policy towards refugees." "We simply can't do any more," the prime minister explained to the nation. When announcing this policy, Åsa Romson—the environment and previous ceremonial deputy prime minister of Sweden, who was one of the two leaders of the Environmental Party—burst into tears.[16] The Environmentalist Party, which believes in free immigration, is struggling to find its way in the new political landscape that has formed following the immigration crises.[17]

Sweden is in a ditch because many politicians, intellectuals and journalists—on both the left and the right—have claimed that refugee immigration is a boon to the country's economy and that large-scale immigration is the only way of sustaining the welfare state. For long, those who criticized this consensus were accused of being narrow-minded and challenge the findings of research. But of course, serious research has never shown that refugee immigrants boost the Swedish economy. The truth is quite the opposite. In May of 2016 Mats Hammarstedt, one of the leading economists in Sweden who has looked at the issue of migration, wrote a report together with Lina Aldén. The paper was published by the prestigious Swedish Fiscal Policy Council, an independent public body that scrutinizes the economic policies of the government. The findings of the report were quite harsh. After the first year of migration, the average refugee creates a net cost of 190,000 Swedish Kronors (over $23,000). As immigrants slowly find work and start contributing to the system, this net loss is reduced five years later, but still stands at the substantial rate of 120,000 Swedish Kronors per year (over $14,500). If there was ever any doubt, there can be none now: refugee immigration to the generous Nordic welfare state creates substantial costs.

I am sure that Sweden will dig itself out of this recent crisis, at least partially. Some challenges, such as crime and poverty in marginalized neighborhoods, are harder to meet. It comes as no surprise that Sweden has moved toward a much higher degree of economic inequality following the influx of immigrants. Sadly, I would wager that this will continue, as many immigrants are simply struggling to find a job, a house, and a meaningful place in society. Perhaps worst of all is the future of children of immigrant origin. Sure, there are those—like my brother and me—who succeed although growing up in immigrant neighborhoods with welfare support. After all, the Swedish welfare state generously funded our education up to doctorate level. However, Sweden's school system has gradually moved from a conservative system, where teachers held power, to a very progressive system where students' liberty is valued highly and teacher authority is frowned upon. This has coincided with a rapid fall in school performance. The PISA global survey has shown that Swedish students' performance went from being close to the average of developed countries in 2000 to significantly below the average in 2012. No other country has experienced such a steep fall. For example, while 13 percent of students in 2000 were low performers in reading, the share had risen to 23 percent in 2012.[18]

Researcher Gabriel Heller Sahlgren has shown that a higher share of immigrant students has contributed to the fall, since many come from families where the parents have little education themselves.[19] However, this is only part of the explanation. Most likely the shift toward progressive teaching methods has led to a gradual fall, which has been ongoing for decades.[20]

The Swedish School Inspectorate has written about the situation of the numerous failing schools where many students of immigrant origin are studying. Its conclusions are quite sad, and clearly show how the lack of teacher authority is destroying the future prospects of many pupils by taking away their chance of getting a good education. A report about Ross Tensta gymnasium, situated in an immigrant neighborhood in Stockholm, reads:

Very severe flaws exist when it comes to safety and a calm study environment. The teachers describe many lessons as chaotic, which the class inspectors of the of the School Inspection can confirm. The School Inspection has observed classes where it is nearly impossible to follow and understand the content of what the teacher is going through. The reason is the inability of the school to deal with students' lack of respect for their teacher and respect for their own and their classmates' learning. Teachers often wind up in conflict with students when they tell students to behave, which leads to a situation where some teachers have given up the ambition to create a calm study environment. Teachers describe situations where teachers can be threatened by students when the latter are told to behave, which leads to teachers in some situations not telling students to stop with negative behavior. This has also led to students being offended by other students without teachers intervening.[21]

School systems without teacher authority where students can harass one another and disturb classes with impunity, where those who wish to study cannot follow the teacher due to a chaotic situation, and where teachers are even afraid of students—haven't we heard this before? Isn't this almost exactly the situation that many public schools in marginalized American neighborhoods, where many children come from marginalized minorities, struggle with? In fact, much of the challenges facing Sweden after the influx of large numbers of immigrants are very much like the situations in such American neighborhoods. As in America, the situation can certainly be turned to the better—by preventing and combating crime, boosting job growth, and turning failing schools around. But the challenges are great. When we take the unique Nordic culture of success out of the equation, by looking at the prospects of immigrant communities, suddenly the Swedish system doesn't seem to be able to solve all social problems. Perhaps this tells us something about the limit of policy, and about the importance of culture for social success?

It remains to be seen if the positive parts of Swedish culture, such as emphasis on individual responsibility, strong social cohesion, and high levels of trust, can be transmitted to the wide immigrant community. I myself believe this to be quite possible with time, at least if the school system, the job market, and crime prevention are all improved. After all, most newcomers to Sweden have a desire to succeed and a genuine interest in the positive parts of Swedish culture (as opposed to the less positive parts, such as the norm of not befriending your neighbors). But it will take time: the Swedish welfare state does not magically transmit social success to all who enter Sweden, Rather, as shown in detail in chapter 9, it is in many ways restricting upward social mobility as compared to the American system. Admirers of Nordic-style social democracy should take a closer look at Sweden's immigration crisis. Only then will they understand that there is a limit on the abilities of social democracy, even in the Nordics, to create social good.

11

WHERE ARE NORDIC SOCIETIES HEADING?

WHERE ARE THE POLICIES IN Nordic societies heading? Certainly, Sweden is engulfed by the immigration crisis we read about in the last chapter. The previously dominant view, that free immigration could be combined with a generous welfare state, is out the window. Swedes might seem a bit strange to Americans, since their society is based on the idea that a consensus should be reached on important social issues. This explains why the only socially acceptable view a few years ago was that borders ought to be open, and why most of the political elite has overnight shifted to the view that immigration should be limited. But of course, the challenge of integrating those immigrants who have already come to Sweden remains. Not only many of the recently arrived immigrants, but also many of the children of immigrants born and raised in Sweden, are struggling to find work and housing. The realization is growing that the Swedish model needs to be changed to allow for greater upward mobility. One big topic is how regulations can be simplified so that more houses can be built. Another is how the entry-level wages can be lowered so that more immigrants can get a job. It is broadly accepted today that the generosity of the welfare system needs to be reduced so that fewer people are trapped in welfare dependency.

A few years ago, admirers of Nordic-style social democracy would often use Sweden as their prime role model. Today, those like Bernie Sanders are increasingly talking about Denmark. The obvious reason is that Sweden has changed. The workfare policies, where taxes and welfare benefits were both reduced, have benefited economic development in Sweden, but also made the country less of a leftist ideal society. The influx of immigrants has led to significant increase in income inequality, poverty, and various other social challenges. Suddenly, the image of an ideal social democratic society is difficult to apply to Sweden. No surprise, then, that Sanders and others on the left are increasingly pointing to Denmark, where taxes and benefits have not been reformed to the same extent as in Sweden, and where governments on both the right and left have favored limited immigration. But change is happening in Denmark too. As we explored previously in this book, even the social democrats in the country openly challenge the idea of an overly generous welfare system.

"Denmark is far from a socialist planned economy. Denmark is a market economy." —DANISH PRIME MINISTER LARS LØKKE RASMUSSEN

After seeing his country held up as an example in the American presidential debate, the current Danish prime minister, Lars Løkke Rasmussen, objected to the skewed image of socialism in his country. In a speech given at Harvard's Kennedy School of Government in late 2015, he told students that he had "absolutely no wish to interfere [with] the presidential debate in the US," but wanted to point out a simple fact: "I know that some people in the US associate the Nordic model with some sort of socialism. Therefore I would like to make one thing clear. Denmark is far from a socialist planned economy. Denmark is a market economy."[1] The remark comes as no surprise. While liberal ideologues in the United States believe that democratic socialism is a flattering label, in the Nordics many object to this. Even the social democrats in the region are distancing themselves from socialist ideas, often pointing out that they, too, embrace the market.

If we systematically look at Nordic countries, we can make a number of observations about the direction of the Nordic-style welfare model. The first is that the generosity of the welfare systems has gradually been reduced. The following table shows the economic situation for an average family with one income-earner and two children who go from work to long-term unemployment. How much is the incentive for the family to return to work compared to remaining on benefits? In the United States a system exists where work is certainly more rewarded than welfare support. The average household would more than double their income by working rather than being supported by welfare. As late as 2001, Nordic countries had a quite different model. The incentives to work were small, and almost nonexistent in Denmark, where benefits would amount to 97 percent of the previous work income, leaving only a measly 3 percent as the reward for work. Since then every country in the Nordics has increased the incentives to work substantially, with the exception of Iceland, where work was already rewarded.

HOW MUCH MORE (PERCENTAGE OF INCOME) WOULD A SINGLE-EARNER FAMILY MAKE BY WORKING COMPARED TO LONG-TERM UNEMPLOYMENT BENEFIT?[2]

	2001	2013 (LATEST AVAILABLE YEAR)	CHANGE
DENMARK	3	21	+ 18
SWEDEN	15	26	+ 11
FINLAND	8	14	+ 6
NORWAY	11	17	+ 6
ICELAND	26	23	-3
UNITED STATES	44	44	+/- 0

Source: OECD and author's calculations. Based on average of net replacement rates over 60 months of unemployment, families qualified for cash household assistance and social assistance "top ups" (for a two-child, one-earner married couple); 2001 is the earliest and 2013 the latest years reported by the OECD.

Sure, Nordic countries still have more generous welfare systems than the United States, but change has indeed taken place lately. During the last decade or so, their systems have moved much closer to the American one, as taxes for working households have been lowered while the benefit levels have been cut. Of course, one could still debate whether it is the American model—which today strongly rewards work—or the Nordic model—which today moderately rewards work—that is best. But if Nordic countries are the judge, their previous model, where work was barely rewarded, is out of the competition. Again, this makes sense. For some time, the Nordic welfare models could rely on the fact that their citizens had unusually strong norms related to work and responsibility. It was therefore feasible to have extremely generous welfare systems, where those who didn't work could be given nearly the same standard of living as those who were working. As people norms gradually adapted to the new system, it became obvious that the social democratic model was eroding personal responsibility and leading to high costs for taxpayers. So the system was changed.

Another recent change is that taxes have been cut. International observers often believe that Nordic people are somehow much more tolerant of high taxes than people who live elsewhere in the world. As noted previously, this is only a half-truth. All Nordic countries have over time moved toward hidden taxation. Around half of the true tax rate is simply hidden from people. If you have a friend in any Nordic country, you can try this for yourself. Ask him how much he pays in taxes, and don't be surprised if his response sounds similar to the taxes paid in the United States.[3] Still, even though taxes are hidden, the Nordic people have been pushing for lower rates.

Bernie Sanders has called for a "political revolution" against "the billionaire class" in America. Of course, he has argued that the role model is Nordic social democracy: "If we know that in countries in Scandinavia, Denmark, Norway, Sweden, they are very democratic countries—the voter turnout is a lot higher than in the United States—and in those countries healthcare is a right, college education and graduate school is free, retirement benefits and childcare benefits are stronger . . . and in those countries government works for ordinary people and the middle class rather than, as is the case right now in our country, for the billionaires."[4] Granted, Nordic societies are somewhat more bent toward high taxes compared to America. But the difference in how much taxes the rich pay is not as large as one would imagine. As shown in the following table, the top tax rate in the United States is actually somewhat higher than in Iceland and Norway, and not much lower than in Denmark, Sweden, and Finland.

> While America has moved toward higher taxes, the Nordic countries have moved towards lower rates.

Also, while America has moved toward higher taxes, the Nordic countries have moved toward lower rates. This is particularly true in Denmark and Norway, where the top income tax rates have been cut by 6.7 and 8.1 percentage points respectively between 2001 and 2014. If an American politician would have suggested this, she or he would likely have been accused of being a pet dog of the billionaire class. In reality, this change has taken place in the Nordics, in two countries which during this period have in part been ruled by social democrat governments. But of course, those who view the Nordic countries through a socialist Shangri-La lens often neglect to note that the very same countries have chosen the path of tax reductions. In Sweden the top rates have been increased somewhat. However, the total taxes have been reduced substantially due to the workfare policies, through which the taxes on low and medium incomes have been substantially cut.

Even most of the rich are paying less taxes in total now, since the reductions of the lower rates also apply to them.

TOP TAX RATE
(INCLUDING SOCIAL SECURITY CONTRIBUTIONS)[5]

	2001	2013 (LATEST AVAILABLE YEAR)	CHANGE
DENMARK	62.3	55.6	- 6.7
SWEDEN	55.5	56.9	+ 1.4
FINLAND	59.1	57.2	- 1.9
NORWAY	55.3	47.2	- 8.1
ICELAND	42.7	44.4	+ 1.7
UNITED STATES	47.4	48.6	+ 1.2

Source: OECD Stat Extract and author's calculations.

Lastly, we can see that the days when the Nordic countries could actually be socialist are long gone. The countries in this part of the world certainly did experiment with democratic socialism during the 1970s. But as we saw previously, the socialist policies that were introduced, particularly in Sweden, proved to be such a failure that they were abandoned after some time. Since then a number of market reforms have been introduced. Denmark has, for example, moved toward quite flexible legislation when it comes to how workers are hired and fired. Sweden has since the 1990s opened up its publicly funded schools, publicly funded health care, and publicly funded elderly care for competition from private businesses. Voucher systems allow private firms to compete with the public sector in providing various forms of welfare. In addition, the Swedish pension system has been partially privatized, giving citizens some control over their mandated retirement savings. Arguably, in these regards Sweden is more of a capitalist country than America is.

The Heritage Foundation each year creates an Index of Economic Freedom in partnership with the *Wall Street Journal.* The index goes through the economic policies of various countries in great detail and scores them accordingly to how free they are. A high score represents a capitalist, free-market system, while a low score represents a system with much government intervention, high taxes, and high public spending. As the following table shows, America has moved toward less economic liberty during the last few years. The Nordic countries, which had come far in adopting capitalism by the beginning of the twenty-first century, have continued to massively strengthen their economic freedom. The only exception is Iceland, which at the turn of the new millennium was already quite a capitalist country. Today the United States is only very marginally more economically free than Denmark. Let's think about this a bit. The United States is barely more capitalist than Denmark. And while America has moved toward less capitalism and higher taxes on the rich, Denmark has moved—much faster—in precisely the opposite direction. Huh. I wonder how often this is acknowledged by those who wish to copy Danish policies in the United States.

Besides having higher taxes and larger public sectors, the Nordic countries are in many other regards more capitalist than America.

In fact, all Nordic countries have a high rate of economic liberty. They are overall just slightly less market-friendly than the United States. This might sound odd to someone who doesn't follow Nordic policies, but in reality makes perfect sense. Capitalism works. And as I have demonstrated in this book, the Nordic experience is very much that free markets create wealth while socialism inhibits job creation and greater prosperity. So, over time the pragmatic Nordic people have introduced a wide range of market policies. Free trade; simple-to-follow regulations for businesses; tax codes that, contrary to the American one, are not full of weird holes; and other market-friendly policies have been introduced. Besides having higher taxes and larger public sectors, the Nordic countries are in many other regards more capitalist than America.

REDUCED SIZE OF GOVERNMENT[6]

ECONOMIC FREEDOM INDEX (HIGH SCORE = MORE CAPITALIST SYSTEM)

	2001	2016 (LATEST AVAILABLE YEAR)	CHANGE
DENMARK	68.3	75.3	+ 7.0
SWEDEN	66.6	72.0	+ 5.4
FINLAND	69.7	72.6	+ 2.9
NORWAY	67.1	70.8	+ 3.7
ICELAND	73.4	73.3	- 0.1
UNITED STATES	79.1	75.4	- 3.7

Source: Index of Economic Freedom and author's calculations.

So there you have it. In America policies are moving toward less capitalism and higher taxes. In the Nordics they are moving toward more capitalism, less generous welfare, and lower taxes. I am not going to say that the experience of the Nordic countries is a proof that America should also move toward a smaller government. But it does show us that even in the part of the world most often used as the proof that socialism actually works, policies are moving from socialism to capitalism. And it shows us that those Americans obsessed with Nordic-style social democracy don't really know much about the policies of the Nordic countries. They are content with viewing the Nordic countries as Utopia. But if we don't disregard these facts, we can learn much from the real Nordic lesson.

In short, the Nordic countries teach us that by having a pragmatic approach, successful welfare state institutions can be introduced. Single-payer health care systems, which avoid much of the bureaucracy and high costs of the American model, public provision of child care that allows many women to work, and public funding of higher education certainly have their merits. The Nordic countries also teach us that high tax rates and attempts to introduce Third Way democratic socialism massively reduce economic performance. Labor market regulations and overly generous welfare policies hinder job creation and create long-lasting welfare dependency. Although well intentioned, the welfare states can through welfare dependency create large obstacles for the poor. This is why the Nordic countries, for all their benefits, are offering fewer opportunities for immigrants to climb the social ladder compared to in America.

And finally, the Nordic countries teach us about the limits of policy. Everything for which the Nordic countries with large welfare states are admired also exists in Iceland, the Nordic cousin with a smaller welfare state. Why? Well, because Iceland has the same culture of success that is the true root of all this success. The same explanation obviously goes for why countries such as Sweden and Denmark achieved high income equality and good social outcomes before introducing large welfare states. And for that matter, why Nordic Americans have much more prosperity and even lower poverty rates than their cousins in the Nordics. To a large extent, the admirers of Nordic society wish to copy Nordic socialism. They fail to realize that what they wish to copy in reality is an extraordinary culture. And they fail to realize that the socialist policies that they so admire have to a large extent been cast aside by the Nordic people themselves.

I don't mind people viewing the Nordics as idealistic, Shangri-La societies. But we should know that there is no such thing as Utopia when it comes to policies, no such thing as a perfect system.

I don't mind people viewing the Nordics as idealistic, Shangri-La societies. If it amuses them, let them. But we should know that there is no such thing as Utopia when it comes to policies, no such thing as a perfect system. There are good reasons to admire parts of Nordic welfare policies, and certainly good reasons to admire the market reforms, tax cuts, and reduced generosity of welfare programs that have been taking place lately in the same countries. What kind of reforms you introduce is all about what kind of goals you want to reach. In this regard there is no difference between America and the Nordic societies. Neither is Utopia. Both have their advantages and disadvantages. And neither of them can simply copy the other, since societies are not formed simply through political mandates. Rather, they are formed through the complex interaction between culture and policies.

So, at the end of the day, the true lesson from the Nordics is this: culture, at least as much as politics, matters. If the goal is to create a better society, we should strive to create a society that fosters a better culture. This can be done by setting up a system wherein people are urged to take responsibility for themselves and their families, trust their neighbors and work together. The Nordic countries did evolve such a culture – during a period when the state was small, when self-reliance was favored. For a time these societies prospered while combining strong norms with a limited welfare state, which was focused on providing services such as education rather than generous handouts. Then came the temptation to increase the size of the welfare state. Slowly a culture of welfare dependency grew, eroding the good norms. So, yes, the Nordics did stumble on a recipe for economic and social success. They did so before turning to large welfare states. Intuitively, it all makes sense. A system that over time encourages work, responsibility and strong families endures and grows stronger. A system that encourages individuals and families to instead rely on the state slowly falters. In this regard, the Nordic nations are anything but exceptional.

Notes

INTRODUCTION

1. Bernie Sanders said this during a Democratic presidential debate on CNN held on October 2015. Moderator Anderson Cooper asked him to elaborate on why he viewed himself as a democratic socialist. Sanders used the Nordic countries as examples of successful democratic socialist models. (CNSNews.com staff, "Bernie Sanders: 'We're Going to Explain What Democratic Socialism Is,'" CNSNews.com, October 15, 2015, http://cnsnews.com/news/article/cnsnewscom-staff/bernie-sanders-were-going-explain-what-democratic-socialism.) The Nordic countries are commonly used as role models by Bernie Sanders and other politicians on the left, in the United States and abroad.

2. Heritage Foundation and *Wall Street Journal*, 2016 Index of Economic Freedom, "Country Rankings," Heritage.org, accessed April 19, 2016, http://www.heritage.org/index/ranking.

3. Blue is the color of the Center Right in most countries, while red is the color of the Center Left. Curiously, the United States has opted for the opposite color scheme.

4. Lisa Hagen, "Rubio: Sanders a Good Candidate for President of Sweden," *Ballot Box* (*The Hill*'s campaign blog), January 28, 2016, http://thehill.com/blogs/ballot-box/presidential-races/267477-rubio-sanders-a-good-candidate-for-president-of-sweden.

5. "Swedish royalists up in arms over US politician's blunder," *The Local*, January 29, 2016, http://www.thelocal.se/20160129/fury-in-sweden-over-marco-rubios-king-blunder

6. Aftonbladet (2015). "Madrasserna slut i hela skåne", 2015-10-08. http://www.aftonbladet.se/nyheter/paflykt/article21550808.ab

7. Sydsvenskan (2016). "Rekordmånga lämnar sina jobb i Malmö stad", 2016-03-29. http://www.sydsvenskan.se/malmo/rekordmanga-lamnar-sina-jobb-i-malmo-stad/. The sick leave number is reported to have been 50 percent for Malmös social emergency service department in the autumn of 2015.

8. "Today's Society Poll of Polls," *Dagens Samhälle* (2016, January 28, 2016, http://www.dagenssamhalle.se/dagens-samhaelle-poll-of-polls. Even when adding the support of the Greens, the total support for the Left is below 40 percent.

9. "*Stefan Löfvens Nya Desperata Krisplan*" (Stefan Löfvens New Desperate Crisis Plan), *Expressen*, February 9, 2016, http://www.expressen.se/nyheter/stefan-lofvens-nya-desperata-krisplan/.

10. The leader of the Swedish Socialists, but not the Social Democrats, has a friendly relationship with Bernie Sanders.

11. This is particularly evident if we look at a key indicator for success later in life: the school results of children from different backgrounds. A shift from conservative to progressive teaching methods has failed pupils from socioeconomically challenged families, particularly migrants. Certainly there is a lesson to be learned here for American observers.

12. Nima Sanandaji, *Scandinavian Unexceptionalism: Culture, Markets and the Failure of Third-Way Socialism* (London: Institute of Economic Affairs, 2015). The book was preceded by the report *The Surprising Ingredients of Swedish Success—Free Markets and Social Cohesion* (Discussion Paper no. 41), which I also wrote for the Institute of Economic Affairs and which came out in 2012 (http://www.iea.org.uk/sites/default/files/publications/files/Sweden%20Paper.pdf); and before that the report "The Swedish Model Reassessed: Affluence Despite the Welfare State," published by Finnish think tank Libera in October 2011, http://www.ncpa.org/sub/dpd/?Article_ID=21268#sthash.HFtMzTp8.dpuf.

CHAPTER 1: AMERICAN OBSESSION WITH NORDIC SOCIAL DEMOCRACY

1. See, for example, Gregory Krieg, "Top Swedish Diplomat Is Not Feeling 'the Bern,'" CNN, February 3, 2016, http://www.cnn.com/2016/02/03/politics/hillary-clinton-bernie-sanders-sweden/.

2. Bernie Sanders, "What Can We Learn from Denmark?" *HuffPost: The Blog*, May 26, 2013, http://www.huffingtonpost.com/rep-bernie-sanders/what-can-we-learn-from-de_b_3339736.html.

3. Ezra Klein, "Bernie Sanders and Hillary Clinton's Debate over Capitalism, Explained," Vox, updated October 14, 2015, http://www.vox.com/2015/10/14/9528873/bernie-sander-hillary-clinton-socialist-debate.

4. "The Swedish Connection," *Washington Times*, June 3, 2015.

5. William J. Clinton, "Remarks to the Citizens of Copenhagen," July 12, 1997, American Presidency Project, http://www.presidency.ucsb.edu/ws/?pid=54410.

6. Bill Clinton, *Back to Work: Why We Need Smart Government for a Strong Economy* (New York: Random House, 2011).

7. Remarks by President Obama and Prime Minister Reinfeldt of Sweden in Joint Press Conference," press release, White House, Office of the Press Secretary, September 4, 2013, https://www.whitehouse.gov/the-press-office/2013/09/04/remarks-president-obama-and-prime-minister-reinfeldt-sweden-joint-press-.

8. Remarks by President Obama, President Niinistö of Finland, and Prime Minister Solberg of Norway at the Nordic Leaders' Summit Arrival Ceremony," press release, White House, Office of the Press Secretary, May 13, 2016, https://www.whitehouse.gov/the-press-office/2016/05/13/remarks-president-obama-president-niinist%C3%B6-finland-and-prime-minister.

9. *"The Boss Vill Göra Amerika Lite Svenskare"* (The Boss Wants to Make America a Bit More Swedish," *Dagens Nyheter*, 2012; Adam Taylor, "Bruce Springsteen Wants the United States to Be More Like Sweden," *Business Insider*, February 17, 2012, http://www.businessinsider.com/bruce-springsteen-sweden-2012-2.

10. "Sweden: Something Souring in Utopia," *Time*, July 19, 1976, http://content.time.com/time/subscriber/article/0,33009,914329-3,00.html.

11. John Logue, "The Welfare State: Victim of Its Success," *Daedalus* 108 no. 4 (Fall 1979): 75.

12. Ibid.; John Logue, "Will Success Spoil the Welfare State? Solidarity and Egotism in Scandinavia." *Dissent*, Winter 1985, 96–104.

13. David Popenoe, "Scandinavian Welfare," *Society* 31, no. 6 (September 1994): 78.

14. Jeffrey D. Sachs, "The Social Welfare State, beyond Ideology," *Scientific American*, November 1, 2006, 42.

15. Paul Krugman, "Socialist Hellhole Blogging," *The Conscience of a Liberal* (*New York Times* blog), August 19, 2011, http://krugman.blogs.nytimes.com/2011/08/19/socialist-hellhole-blogging/.

16. Derrick Z. Jackson, "Memo to Hillary Clinton: What's Not to Like about Denmark?" *Boston Globe*, October 19, 2015, https://www.bostonglobe.com/opinion/2015/10/19/memo-hillary-clinton-what-not-like-about-denmark/PoV2OD3KpysMFCAz2XLI0K/story.html.

17. "Nobel Nucléaire," *Le Monde*, August 10, 2005.

18. Shangri-La is a fictional place described in the 1933 novel *Lost Horizon*, written by British author James Hilton. Hilton describes it as a mystical, harmonious valley. Rich Lowry recently used Shangri-La as an analogue for the American Left's view of Nordic welfare states in his article "Sorry, Bernie—Scandinavia Is No Socialist Paradise after All," *New York Post*, October 19, 2015, http://nypost.com/2015/10/19/sorry-bernie-scandinavia-is-no-socialist-paradise-after-all/.

19. OECD, Better Life Index–Edition 2015, OECD.Stat, http://stats.oecd.org/Index.aspx?DataSetCode=BLI. The analysis is based on the default settings on the index, where the different sub-indexes are measured equally. The Nordic countries also ranked high in previous editions of the same index. See, for example, *Huffington Post* Canada, "Canada Ranks Fifth On OECD's Better Life Index," *Huffington Post*, May 5, 2014, http://www.huffingtonpost.ca/2014/05/05/canada-better-life-index_n_5269677.html; and "Australia Ranked 'Happiest' Developed Nation Again," BBC News, May 28, 2013, http://www.bbc.com/news/business-22685260.

20. Save the Children, *The Urban Disadvantage: State of the World's Mothers 2015* (Fairfield, CT: Save the Children, 2015), 9, http://www.savethechildren.org/atf/cf/%7B9def2ebe-10ae-432c-9bd0-df91d2eba74a%7D/SOWM_EXECUTIVE_SUMMARY.PDF.

CHAPTER 2: NORDIC SUCCESS PREDATES LARGE WELFARE STATES

1. *Field of Dreams*, directed by Phil Alden Robinson (Universal City, CA: Universal Pictures, 1989). Film.

2. Henrik Jacobsen Kleven, "How Can Scandinavians Tax So Much?," *Journal of Economic Perspectives* 28, no. 4 (Fall 2014): 96, http://pubs.aeaweb.org/doi/pdfplus/10.1257/jep.28.4.77.

3. Based on my calculations using the latest available data (2014) from OECD.Stat, the standard of living among Icelanders is 81 percent as high as in the United States, while that of Sweden and Denmark is 83 and 85 percent, respectively, as high. Thanks to the oil, Norwegians are 19 percent more affluent than Americans. Finns have 75 percent of the prosperity of Americans, although their country, like Sweden and Norway, has massive forestry resources. See the data for GDP per head of population. USD, current prices, current PPPs, at http://stats.oecd.org/, accessed February 9, 2016.

4. In 1960 the total tax rate in the United States was 27 percent. This is comparable with the Nordic countries, as the tax rate was 25 percent in Denmark, 28 percent in Finland, 29 percent in Sweden, and 32 per cent in Norway. "Government Tax and Revenue Chart," usgovernmentrevenue, accessed April 20, 2016, http://www.usgovernmentrevenue.com/revenue_chart_1900_2020USp_F0fF0sF0l; Nordic data is from the Swedish Tax Agency's (Skatteverket) "Tax Statistical Yearbook of Sweden 2007." Historic data for Iceland is difficult to find.

5. In 2000 taxes amounted to 28 percent of GDP in the United States, lower than in Iceland, with a 36 percent rate, and much lower than in Norway (42 percent), Finland (46 percent), Denmark (47 percent), and Sweden (49 percent). OECD, "Revenue Statistics—Comparative tables," OECD.Stat, accessed February 9, 2016, http://stats.oecd.org/Index.aspx?DataSetCode=REV.

6. Associated Press, "What Can the U.S. Learn from Denmark?" *The Rundown* (PBS blog), October 15, 2015, http://www.pbs.org/newshour/rundown/can-u-s-learn-denmark/.

7. Based on calculations gathered from the World Bank World Development Indicators Database, accessed February 7, 2016. See http://databank.worldbank.org/data/reports.aspx?source=world-development-indicators.

8. usgovernmentrevenue.com and the Swedish Tax Agency (2007).

9. World Bank World Development Indicators Database.

10. Under-five mortality rate for 2015. UN Inter-agency Group for Child Mortality Estimation (IGME), Child Mortality Estimates, http://www.childmortality.org, data gathered February 7, 2016.

11. Jesper Roine and Daniel Waldenström, "The Evolution of Top Incomes in an Egalitarian Society; Sweden, 1903–2004," *Journal of Public Economics* 92, nos. 1–2 (2008): 366.

12. A. B. Atkinson and J. E. Søgaard, "The Long-Run History of Income Inequality in Denmark: Top Incomes from 1870 to 2010" (2013), EPRU Working Paper Series, Department of Economics, University of Copenhagen, available for download at https://ideas.repec.org/p/kud/epruwp/13-01.html.

13. Tino Sanandaji, "Poverty and Causality," *Critical Review* 24, no. 1 (2012): 56–57.

14. One of the reasons that children's incomes are related to those of their parents is that general differences exist between subgroups within society. Studies that have decomposed mobility find that more than half of the intergenerational correlation in the United States is due to persistence of earnings differences across racial and ethnic groups. See Tom Hertz, "A Group-Specific Measure of Intergenerational Persistence," *Economics Letters* 100, no. 3 (September 2008): 415–17.

15. OECD Stat Extract. Latest available data for the year 2014, http://stats.oecd.org/.

CHAPTER 3: COFFEE-CONSUMING WORKAHOLICS

1. Trygve Gulbrandsen, for example, found that over 90 percent of Norwegian managers in both the private and the public sector agree that laws giving employers influence over businesses are advantageous for Norwegian working life. Gulbrandsen, "Elite Integration and Institutional Trust in Norway," *Comparative Sociology* 6 (2007): 190–214, https://www.duo.uio.no/bitstream/handle/10852/15204/EliteintISS.pdf?sequence=1. See also Peter B. Smith et al., "In Search of Nordic Management Styles," *Scandinavian Journal of Management* 19, no. 4 (2003): 491–507; and Tor Grenness, "*På Jakt Etter en Norsk Ledelsesmodell*" (In Search of a Norwegian *management model*), *Magma* (2012): 51–59, http://www.magma.no/pa-jakt-etter-en-norsk-ledelsesmodell.

2. Marie-joelle Browaeys and Roger Price, *Understanding Cross-Cultural Management* (Essex, UK: Prentice Hall, 2008).

3. See, for example, Birte Siim and Pauline Stoltz, "Particularities of the Nordic: Challenges to Equality Politics in a Globalized World," in Stine Thidemann Faber and Helene Pristed Nielsen, eds., *Remapping Gender, Place and Mobility: Global Confluences and Local Particularities in Nordic Peripheries (Gender in a Global/Local World)* (London and New York: Routledge, 2015), chap 2.

4. Kelly Services, "Company Loyalty and Employee Engagement in the Workforce—A European Perspective: 2010 Kelly Global Workforce Index," http://www.slideshare.net/MicKir/company-loyalty-and-employee-engagement-report-4471514.

5. Richard R. Gesteland, *Cross-Cultural Business Behavior: A Guidebook for Those Who Work in Different Countries*, 5th rev. ed. (Copenhagen Business School Press, 2012).

6. David Kamp, "The Hacker and the Hack," *New York Times Sunday Book Review*, May 28, 2010, http://www.nytimes.com/2010/05/30/books/review/Kamp-t.html?pagewanted=all.

7. Roberto Ferdman, "Here Are the Countries That Drink the Most Coffee—the U.S. Isn't in the Top 10," *Atlantic*, January 15, 2014, http://www.theatlantic.com/business/archive/2014/01/here-are-the-countries-that-drink-the-most-coffee-the-us-isnt-in-the-top-10/283100/.

8. International Coffee Council, *Trends in Coffee Consumption in Selected Importing Countries*, September 2012, http://www.ico.org/documents/icc-109-8e-trends-consumption.pdf.

9. Taija Ojaniemi ""Coffee as a Finnish Institution": A FAST-FIN-1 (TRENAK1) Finnish Institutions Research Paper, Department of Translation Studies, University of Tampere (2010), http://www15.uta.fi/FAST/FIN/GEN/to-coffe.html.

10. Ibid.

11. See, for example, R. H. Nelson, "Max Weber Revisited," in Ilkka Pyysiäinen, ed., *Religion, Economy, and Cooperation* (n.p.: De Gruyter, 2010).

12. Assar Lindbeck, "Hazardous Welfare-State Dynamics," *American Economic Review* 85, no 2 (1995): 9–15; Assar Lindbeck, "An Essay on Welfare State Dynamics," CESifo Working Paper Series no. 976 (May 15, 2003), http://www.ifn.se/Wfiles/wp/WP595.pdf.

13. Quoted in R. W. McColl, ed., *Encyclopedia of World Geography* ("political geography").

14. Denmark is the only Nordic nation that adopted a feudal system where most farmworkers were landless and also limited from seeking employment on a free labor market. The result was that farmers had little incentives to work hard to produce the food. During the late eighteenth century and onward, Denmark begun moving toward a system of independent farmers, which opened the path to increased prosperity.

15. Jefferson made this remark in 1781, a few years after playing a key role in writing the Declaration of Independence and two decades before becoming the third president of the new nation. Merrill Peterson, ed., *Jefferson Writings* (New York: Literary Classics of the U.S., 1984), 301.

16. The poem "Saarijarven Paavo" and description of the circumstances relating to its writing appear in Lars Huldén, ed., *Johan Ludvig Runeberg Dikter* (Stockholm: Atlantis, 1998).

17. *The Treasury of Knowledge and Library of Reference, Parts I., II., and III.*, 5th ed., s.v. "Sweden." Similarly, a source from the early nineteenth century explains, "[Swedes] are brave, sober, patient, pliable, well-principled, and industrious." John Joseph Stockdale, *The History of Gustavus Adolphus, King of Sweden, Surnamed the Great*, 3rd ed., vol. 1 (London: Hausard, 1807), 212.

18. Conrad Malte-Brun, *Universal Geography*, vol. 2 (Boston: S. Walker, 1834).

19. Andrew Crichton and Henry Wheaton, *Scandinavia, Ancient and Modern, Being a History of Denmark, Sweden and Norway*, vol. 2 (Edinburgh: Oliver & Boyd, 1838), 341.

20. Jan Delhy and Kenneth Newton, "Predicting Cross-National Levels of Social Trust: Global Patterns or Nordic Exceptionalism?," *European Sociological Review* 21 (2005): 311–27; Niclas Berggren, Mikael Elinder, and Henrik Jordahl, "Trust and Growth: A Shaky Relationship," Empirical Economics 35 (2008): 251–74.

21. Delhy and Newton, 311.

22. In a paper Daniel Arnold looks at the link between benefit morale and the generosity of sick pay entitlements. Benefit morale is measured through the World Value Survey, a global attitude study where respondents are asked if they believe it can sometimes be justified to claim government benefits to which they are not entitled. By examining

thirty-one different developed economies between 1981 and 2010, Arnold can show that countries with high benefit morale have fewer using the sick leave, indicating that overutilization is directly affected by morale. Daniel Arnold, "Benefit Morale and Cross-Country Diversity in Sick Pay Entitlement," *Kyklos* 66 (2013): 27–45.

23. See Eric M. Uslaner, "Where You Stand Depends upon Where Your Grandparents Sat: The Inheritability of Generalized Trust," *Public Opinion Quarterly* 72, no. 4 (2008): 725–40; Tino Sanandaji, "Proving Bo Rothstein Wrong: Why Do Swedes Trust More? Culture, Not Welfare State Policy," blog of Tino Sanandaji, October 2, 2010, http://www.tino.us/2010/10/proving-bo-rothstein-wrong-why-do-swedes-trust-more-culture-not-welfare-state-policy/.

24. Andreas Bergh and Christian Bjørnskov, "Historical Trust Levels Predict the Current Size of the Welfare State," *Kyklos* 64, no. 1 (February 2011): 1.

CHAPTER 4: COMPARING APPLES TO APPLES

1. H. Arnold Barton, "Swedes and Swedish Americans, 1870–1940," in *Immigrants in American History: Arrival, Adaptation, and Integration*, vol. 1, Elliott Robert Barkan, ed. (Santa Barbara: ABC-CLIO. 2013), 631.

2. Eric Dregni, *Vikings in the Attic: In Search of Nordic America* (Minneapolis: University of Minnesota Press, 2011), 174.

3. Rebecca J. Mead, *Swedes in Michigan* (East Lansing: Michigan State University Press, 2012).

4. David Macaray, "The Man Who Saved a Billion Lives," *WorldPost*, October 15, 2013, http://www.huffingtonpost.com/david-macaray/the-man-who-saved-a-billi_b_4099523.html.

5. According to the American Community Survey (ACS) of 2013, there are 4.5 million Norwegian Americans; 4 million Swedish Americans; 1.3 million Danish Americans; 640,000 Finnish Americans; and 580,000 Scandinavian Americans. United States Census Bureau, American Community Survey, "Selected Population Profile in the United States," based on 2013 data.

6. OECD Stat Extract. Level of GDP per Capita and Productivity. Data gathered January 13, 2016.

7. One study compares Norwegians who migrated to the United States from urban areas with those who stayed in Norway. It finds that the Norwegians who sailed to America tended to face poorer economic conditions than those who stayed behind. See Ran Abramitzky, Leah Platt Boustan, and Katherine Eriksson, "Europe's Tired, Poor, Huddled Masses: Self-Selection and Economic Outcomes in the Age of Mass Migration," *American Economic Review* 102, no. 5 (2012): 1832–56.

8. The American Community Survey gives data for the share of those twenty-five or older who are high school graduates or have a higher education. This is compared with data from Eurostat for twenty-five-to-seventy-four-year olds who have the

equivalent education level. Eurostat database (http://ec.europa.eu/eurostat/data/ database), Population by Educational Attainment Level, Sex and Age (%), data gathered January 13, 2016.

9.   These calculations are based on the estimation that the income levels of Nordic American subgroups correspond to their contribution to United States GDP.

10. The American Community Survey gives data for the share of those sixteen or older who are unemployed. The corresponding OECD data also includes fifteen-year-olds.

11. OECD Stat Extract. Short-Term Labor Market Statistics. Unemployment Rates by Age and Gender, %. All people. Data gathered January 13, 2016.

12. Geranda Notten and Chris de Neubourg, "Monitoring Absolute and Relative Poverty: 'Not Enough' Is Not the Same as 'Much Less,'" *Review of Income and Wealth* 57, NO. 2 (2011): 247–69. Norway was not included in the study, since it is not a European Union member state.

13. In part this may be because immigrants to Nordic countries have relatively high poverty rates.

14. Joel Kotkin, "Is Obama Separating from His Scandinavian Muse?" New Geography, December 11, 2009, http://www.newgeography.com/content/001260-our-president-accolades-abroad-tone-deaf-home.

CHAPTER 5: HOW CAN THE NORDICS TAX SO MUCH?

1.   Henrik Jacobsen Kleven, "How Can Scandinavians Tax So Much?" *Journal of Economic Perspectives* 28, no. 4 (Fall 2014): 77–98. Lately the Nordic tax rates have been reduced somewhat.

2.   Mathias Trabandt and Harald Uhlig, "How Far Are We from the Slippery Slope? The Laffer Curve Revisited" (working paper, European Central Bank Working Paper Series no 1174, 2010), https://www.ecb.europa.eu/pub/pdf/scpwps/ecbwp1174.pdf?344d6e7 7a58718332bd900b10e4d85b2. Norway is not included in the analysis since it is not part of the European Union. Iceland is not included either, since it is a small country.

3.   See, for example, Bertil Holmlund and Martin Söderström, "Estimating Income Responses to Tax Changes: A Dynamic Panel Data Approach" (IZA Discussion Paper Series, no. 3088, 2007, http://ftp.iza.org/dp3088.pdf).

4.   That is to say, the economy shrinks with three kronor, while one krona is transferred from the private to the public sector. Åsa Hansson, "Vad Kostar Beskattning—Analys av den Samhällsekonomiska Kostnaden av Beskattning," Confederation of Swedish Enterprise, September 4, 2009.

5.   We can do the calculation ourselves. Out of 132 kronor, 32 are paid in payroll tax, leaving 100 kronor. Then 32 + 25 = 57 percent are paid in municipal and state taxes, leaving 43 kronor. Then 21 / 121 = 17 percent of 43 kronor, which equals 7 kronor, is paid in consumption tax, leaving 36 kronor. In total, 96 kronor is paid to the tax agency, which is 73 percent of the original sum of 132 kronor.

6. Jukka Pirttilä and Hakkan Selin, "Skattepolitik och sysselsättning: Hur väl fungerar det svenska systemet?" (appendix 12), in *Långtidsutredningen* 2011 (2011).

7. Peter Ericson and Lennart Flood, "*Höjda Eller Sänkta Marginalskatter för Mer Resurser Till Skolan?*" (Raising or Lowering Marginal Taxes for More Resources to School?) Confederation of Swedish Enterprise, April 16, 2014, http://www.svensktnaringsliv. se/material/rapporter/hojda-eller-sankta-marginalskatter-for-mer-resurser-till-skolan_585927.html.

8. See, for example, Mads Lundby Hansen, "Det Private Forbrug Pr. Inbygger Ligger Nr. 14 i OECD—En Nedgang fra en 6. Plads 1970," CEPOS, December 5, 2012, http:// www.altinget.dk/misc/Notat_Det%20private%20forbrug%20pr.%20indbygger%20 ligger%20nr.%2014%20i%20OECD%20-%20en%20nedgang%20fra%20en%20 6%20plads%20i%201970_dec12.pdf.

9. Ibid.

10. Kleven, "How Can Scandinavians Tax So Much?"

11. Philipp Doerrenberg et al., "Nice Guys Finish Last: Do Honest Taxpayers Face HigherTax Rates?," *Kyklos* 67, no. 1 (February 2014): 29-53. Available online at http:// dx.doi.org/10.1111/kykl.12042,

12. S. H. Baker, "The Determinants of Median Voter Tax Liability: An Empirical Test of the Fiscal Illusion Hypothesis," *Public Finance Quarterly* 11, no. 1, (1983): 95–108.

13. James M. Buchanan, *Fiscal Theory and Political Economy: Selected Essays*, 2nd ed. (Chapel Hill: University of North Carolina Press, 1960).

14. Bertil Ohlin, "Ny 'Osynlig' Moms," *Dagens Nyheter*, March 28, 1973.

15. Tino Sanandaji and Björn Wallace, "Fiscal Illusion and Fiscal Obfuscation—Tax Perception in Sweden," *Independent Review* 16, no. 2 (Fall 2011): 237–46. This is in line with international studies about indirect taxation. Jean-Robert Tyran and Rupert Sausgruber, for example, show that "tax burden associated with an indirect tax is systematically underestimated, whereas this is not the case with an equivalent direct tax." Tyran and Sausgruber, "Testing the Mill Hypothesis of Fiscal Illusion," *Public Choice* 122, no. 1 (2005): 39–68.

16. Particularly the young had a limited knowledge about the actual rate. Two-thirds of young respondents believed that the tax rate was 30 percent or less. Nima Sanandaji, "*Underskattade Skatter—en Undersökning av vad Svenska Folket Tror om Skatternas Omfattning*" (Understated Taxes—an Examination of What the Swedish People Think about Taxes Extent), Confederation of Swedish Enterprise, August 2015, http://www. svensktnaringsliv.se/material/rapporter/underskattade-skatter-en-undersokning-av-vad-svenska-folket-tror_624361.html. The first survey in 2003 was carried out by my brother Tino Sanandaji and his coauthor, Björn Wallace, while I conducted the follow-up survey in 2015. Both surveys influenced the debate about taxation in Sweden.

CHAPTER 6: THE NORDIC FREE-MARKET SUCCESS STORY, AND THE FAILURE OF

THIRD WAY SOCIALISM

1. David Kenstenbaum, "Denmark Thrives Despite High Taxes," NPR, January 29, 2010, http://www.npr.org/templates/story/story.php?storyId=123126942.

2. Subhash Thakur et al., *Sweden's Welfare State: Can the Bumblebee Keep Flying?* (Washington, DC: International Monetary Fund, 2003).

3. J. P. Beddy, "A Comparison of the Principal Economic Features of Eire and Denmark," *Journal of the Statistical and Social Inquiry Society of Ireland* 27 (1943): 189–220.

4. Ibid.

5. K. O'Rourke, "Late Nineteenth Century Denmark in an Irish Mirror: Land Tenure, Homogeneity and the Roots of Danish Success," in J. C. Campbell, A. Hall, and O. Pedersen, eds., *The State of Denmark: Small States, Corporatism and the Varieties of Capitalism* (Montreal: McGill-Queen's University Press, 2006).

6. K. H. O'Rourke, "Property Rights, Social Cohesion and Innovation: Evidence from the Creameries," mimeo, Trinity College, Dublin, 2003.

7. See, for example, Hull Kristensen, "Denmark: An Experimental Laboratory for New Industrial Models," *Entrepreneurship & Regional Development* 1, no. 3 (1989): 245–55.

8. Nima Sanandaji, "Entreprenörer som går mot strömmen. Vad 90-talskrisens succéföretagare kan lära om dagens utman-ingar," Fores, 2010.

9. Based on author calculations and A. Maddison, "Historical Statistics of the World Economy: 1–2008 AD" (2010), data file downloaded April 21, 2016, from http://www.ggdc.net/maddison/Historical_Statistics/horizontal-file_02-2010.xls.

10. Ibid.

11. "What Makes Nordic Countries the Envy of the World," *Economist*, February 2, 2013.

12. M. Henrekson, "Välfärdsstaten och Entreprenörskapet," IFN Policy Paper no. 16 (2007).

13. S. Axelsson, "Entreprenören från sekelskifte till sekelskifte—kan företag växa i Sverige?", in Dan Johansson and Nils Karlsson, eds., *Svensk utvecklingskraft* (Stockholm, Ratio, 2006). In 2004, thirty-eight of the one hundred businesses with the highest revenues in Sweden were entrepreneurial, that is to say, started as privately owned businesses within the country. Of these firms, twenty-one were founded before 1913. Additionally, fifteen were founded between 1914 and 1970. Only two had been formed after 1970. If the one hundred largest firms are instead ranked according to how many people they employed, none of the largest entrepreneurial firms were founded after 1970.

14. See, for example, A. Lindbeck, "The Swedish Experiment," *Journal of Economic Literature* 35 (1997): 1273–1319.

15. Based on author calculations and Maddison, "Historical Statistics."

16. Based on author's calculations and from the OECD Stat Extract. Growth in GDP per capita, productivity and ULC. GDP per capita, constant prices. Data downloaded February 16, 2016.

17. Shortly before the transfer of power to the new reformist government, the Swedish business daily *Dagens Industri* had a headline reading, "Sweden Is the World Champion in 'Jobless Growth.'" "*Sverige världsmästare i* 'jobless growth,'" *Dagens Industri*, January 27, 2006.

18. Carl Magnus Bjuggren and Dan Johansson, "*Privat* och offentlig sysselsättning i Sverige 1950–2005" (Private and Public Employment in Sweden 1950–2005), Ekonomisk Debatt (Economic Debate) 1, no. 1 (2009): 41–53; Frida Nannesson, "Privat och Offentlig Sysselsättning" (Private and Public Employment), Ekonomifakta, data gathered February 16, 2016, from http://www.ekonomifakta.se/sv/Fakta/Arbetsmarknad/Sysselsattning/Privat-och-offentlig-sysselsattning--historiskt/.

19. Olle Krantz, "*Svensk ekonomisk tillväxt under 1900–talet—en problematisk historia*" (Swedish Economic Growth during the 1900s—a Problematic History) *Ekonomisk Debatt*, no 1. (1997), http://www.nationalekonomi.se/filer/pdf/28-1-ok.pdf.

20. See, for example, Anders Johnson, "Tidernas entreprenörer i Sverige," Gleerups Utbildning (2006).

21. Ola Honningdal Grytten, "Why Was the Great Depression Not so Great in the Nordic Countries?: Economic Policy and Unemployment," *Journal of European Economic History* 37, no. 2/3 (2008): 369–93, 395–403. One explanation is that Nordic countries had had a crisis before the Great Depression, which partially prepared them for what was to come.

22. "Arbetskraftsundersökningar (AKU)" (Labour Force Survey [LFS]), http://www.scb.se/AKU/; Statistics Sweden, 2009, Sysselsättningen i Sverige [Employment in Sweden] 1963–2008.

23. Kalle Bengtsson, Claes Ekström, and Diana Farrell, "Sweden's Growth Paradox," *McKinsey Quarterly* (June 2006): 6, http://www.workforall.org/assets/Sweden_GrowthParadox.pdf.

24. Seppo Honkapohja Erkki Koskela, "The Economic Crisis of the 1990s in Finland," *Economic Policy* 14, no. 29 (October 1999): 399–436.

25. Klas Fregert and Jaakko Pehkonen, "Causes of Structural Unemployment in Finland and Sweden 1990–2004," in Lars Jonung, Jaakko Kiander, and Pentti Vartia, eds., *The Crisis of the 1990s in Finland and Sweden: The Nordic Experience of Financial Liberalization* (Northampton, MA: Edward Elgar, 2008).

26. Bengtsson, Ekström, and Farrell, "Sweden's Growth Paradox," 5. The report notes that the government at the time only counted 239,000 individuals as unemployed but that additionally 106,000 people were on government labor market programs. There were also 140,000 so-called "latent job candidates," individuals who were classified as not being in the labor force but who wanted to work and could start working within 14 days (e.g. full-time students who would rather work). Including these groups, the unemployment number would have risen to 485,000 (10 percent of the labor force). Additionally, Sweden had 132,000 under employed individuals and 215,000 people able to work but excluded from the official labor force statistics. The latter figure included

people in early retirement or on prolonged sick leave beyond Sweden's normal historic levels from the 1970s. Adding all above groups, the total unemployment figure was found to be fully 832,000, or 17 percent of the labor force (p. 5, exhibit 4).

27. Jan Edling, *Alla Behövs: Blott Arbetsmarknadsåtgärder Skapar Inga nya Jobb* (2005), http://www.timbro.se/pdf/Alla_behovs_2.pdf; *Agenda för Sverige* (2005), http://aof.nu/Agendaf%C3%B6rSverige.pdf.

28. See for example Confederation of Swedish Enterprise (2006) and Herin et al. (2006).

29. Lars Ljungqvist and Thomas J. Sargent, "Hur Sveriges arbetslöshet blev mer lik Europas," in NBER report *Att Reformera Välfärdsstaten: Amerikanskt Perspektiv på den Svenska Modellen* (Reforming the Welfare State: American Perspective on the Swedish Model), by Richard B. Freeman, Birgitta Swedenborg, Robert Topel, eds. (Stockholm: SNS Förlag, 2006), 109–22, http://www.sns.se/sites/default/files/kr-2006-rapport.pdf.

30. Susanne Spector, "Den verkliga arbetslöshetens utveckling sedan 1996," Confederation of Swedish Enterprise, 2014, http://www.svensktnaringsliv.se/migration_catalog/Rapporter_och_opinionsmaterial/Rapporter/den-verkliga-arbetsloshetens-utveckling_599841.html/binary/Den%20verkliga%20arbetsl%C3%B6shetens%20utveckling. In 2013, the latest available year, it was 14 percent, compared with the official statistics of 8 percent.

CHAPTER 7: WHY ARE SO FEW NORDIC WOMEN AT THE TOP?

1. Many respond that women have advantages in terms of being organized and compassionate leaders. Pew Research Center, "Women and Leadership," January 14, 2015, http://www.pewsocialtrends.org/2015/01/14/women-and-leadership/.

2. World Economic Forum, "The Global Gender Gap Report 2014," http://reports.weforum.org/global-gender-gap-report-2014/.

3. Saadia Zahidi, "What Makes the Nordic Countries Gender Equality Winners?," *HuffPost Impact: The Blog*, October 24, 2013 http://www.huffingtonpost.com/saadia-zahidi/what-makes-the-nordic-cou_b_4159555.html.

4. Katrin Bennhold, "In Sweden, Men Can Have It All," *New York Times*, June 9, 2010, http://www.nytimes.com/2010/06/10/world/europe/10iht-sweden.html?_r-0.

5. Agence France-Presse, "Swedish Fathers to Get Third Month of Paid Paternity Leave," *Guardian*, May 28, 2015, http://www.theguardian.com/world/2015/may/28/swedish-fathers-paid-paternity-parental-leave.

6. Gabrielle Jackson, "Force Men to Take Paternity Leave. It Will Make the World a Better Place," *Guardian*, April 9, 2015, http://www.theguardian.com/commentisfree/2015/apr/10/want-better-dads-happier-mums-and-healthier-kids-make-men-take-paternity-leave.

7. During the battle of Dorostolon, Kievian Rus forces—who were essentially Swedish Vikings with a strong presence in today's Russia—invaded present-day Bulgaria. A counteroffensive by the Byzantine Empire dealt a devastating defeat to the Vikings. The Byzantine were stunned at discovering armed women among their fallen enemies. D. Harrison and K. Svensson, *Vikingaliv* (Fälth & Hässler, 2007).

8.   See Marianne Moen, "The Gendered Landscape: A Discussion on Gender, Status and Power Expressed in the Viking Age Mortuary Landscape" (master's dissertation, University of Oslo, 2010), 5, 30, https://www.duo.uio.no/bitstream/handle/10852/23050/ThexGenderedxLandscape.pdf?sequence=2.

9.   Anders Johnson, *De gjorde skillnad: liberala kvinnor från Anna Maria Lenngren till Marit Paulsen* (Stockholm: Folkpartiet Liberalerna, 2011).

10.   Kari Melby, Anna-Birte Ravn, and Christina Carlsson Wetterberg, *Gender Equality and Welfare Politics in Scandinavia: The Limits of Political Ambition?* (Bristol, UK: Policy Press, 2009).

11.   Anita Lignell Du Rietz, *Svenskornas Företagsamma Historia* [Swedish Hosts Enterprising History] (Stockholm: Timbro, 2009).

12.   Based on information taken from the International Labour Organization, Women in Business and Management Gaining Momentum (ILO, 2015), http://www.ilo.org/wcmsp5/groups/public/---dgreports/---dcomm/---publ/documents/publication/wcms_334882.pdf.

13.   Eurostat, "The European Structure of Earnings Survey," 1995.

14.   T. Iversen, F. Rosenbluth, and D. Soskice "Women and the Service Sector," memo for UCLA Postindustrial Working Group, April 18–19, 2004.

15.   Magnus Henrekson and Mikael Stenkula, "Why Are There So Few Female Top Executives in Egalitarian Welfare States?" *Independent Review* 14, no. 2 (Fall 2009): 243, 264, https://www.independent.org/pdf/tir/tir_14_02_05_henrekson.pdf.

16.   Monica Renstig, "Equal Opportunities in Sweden? Women Can Have a job but Forget The Career," in *Alexander Hughes European Newsletter* no. 31, 2008.

17.   Richard Anker, *Gender and Jobs: Sex Segregation of Occupations in the World* (Geneva: International Labour Office, 1998), 48; emphasis in original.

18.   Nordic Innovation Centre, *Women Entrepreneurship—A Nordic Perspective* (Oslo: Nordic Innovation Centre, 2007), 12–13, http://www.nordicinnovation.org/Global/_Publications/Reports/2007/women_entrepreneurship_final_report_web.pdf.

19.   Matti Alestalo, Sven E. O. Hort, and Stein Kuhnle, *The Nordic Model: Conditions, Origins, Outcomes, Lessons* (Hertie School of Governance Working Paper no. 41, June 2009), 16, https://www.hertie-school.org/fileadmin/images/Downloads/working_papers/41.pdf.

20.   M. Lundbäck, for example, shows that public ventures are worse at implementing innovations and increase their efficiency compared to private firms. Lundback, "Vinster av konkurrenssättning av den offentliga sektorn," in *Den svenska tillväxtskolan: om den ekonomiska utvecklingens kreativa förstörelse* (The Swedish Growth School: Of the Economic Development of Creative Destruction), eds. Dan Johansson and Nils Karlsson (Stockholm: Ratio, 2002).

21.   Eva M. Meyersson Milgrom, Trond Petersen, and Vemund Snartland, "Equal Pay for Equal Work? Evidence from Sweden and a Comparison with Norway and the U.S." *Scandinavian Journal of Economics* 103, no. 4. (December 2001): 559–83.

22. OECD, *Government at a Glance 2015* (OECD, 2015).

23. The Swedish Agency for Public Management, *Den offentliga sektorn i korthet 2014* (STATKONTORET, 2014).

24. Johan Kreicbergs and Carl Oreland, "*Nyföretagande inom den offentliga sektorn—ett lyft för kvinnor*" (Business creation in the public sector— a raise for employees), Svenskt Näringsliv (2009), http://www.svensktnaringsliv.se/migration_catalog/Rapporter_och_opinionsmaterial/Rapporters/nyforetagande-inom-den-offentliga-sektorn-ett-lonelyft-for-de-ans_529836.html/BINARY/Nyf%C3%B6retagande%20inom%20den%20offentliga%20sektorn%20-%20ett%20l%C3%B6nelyft%20f%C3%B6r%20de%20anst%C3%A4llda.

25. Julia Dawson, Richard Kersley, and Stefano Natella, *The CS Gender 3000: Women in Senior Management* (Zurich: Credit Suisse Research Institute, 2014).

26. Kenneth R. Ahern and Amy K. Dittmar, "The Changing of the Boards: The Impact on Firm Valuation of Mandated Female Board Representation," *Quarterly Journal of Economics*, 127, no. 1. (2012): 137–97.

27. Marianne Bertrand et al. "Breaking the Glass Ceiling? The Effect of Board Quotas on Female Labor Market Outcomes in Norway" (National Bureau of Economic Research Working Paper No. 20256, 2014), 2, https://www.utexas.edu/cola/_files/jd25763/norway_boards_5_2014.pdf.

28. "Norway's Female Boardroom Quotas: What Has Been the Effect?" *Nordic Labour Journal* (May 21, 2015).

CHAPTER 8: GENEROUS WELFARE TRAPS FAMILIES IN WELFARE POVERTY

1. Franklin D. Roosevelt, Annual Message to Congress, January 4, 1935, American Presidency Project, accessed February 16, 2016, http://www.presidency.ucsb.edu/ws/?pid=14890.

2. See Friedrich Heinemann, "Is the Welfare State Self-Destructive? A Study of Government Benefit Morale," Discussion Paper No. 07-029 (ZEW [Centre for European Economic Research], 2008), http://ftp.zew.de/pub/zew-docs/dp/dp07029.pdf; *Kyklos* 61, no. 2 (2008): 237–57.

3. Erns Fehr and Urs Fischbacher, "Social Norms and Human Cooperation," *Trends in Cognitive Sciences* 4 (2004): 185–90.

4. Heinemann, "Is the Welfare State Self-Destructive?"

5. Ronald Reagan, Radio Address to the Nation on Welfare Reform, February 15 1986, American Presidency Project, accessed February 16, 2016, http://www.presidency.ucsb.edu/ws/?pid=36875.

6. Ibid.

7. Heinemann, "Is the Welfare State Self-Destructive?"

8. World Value Survey data for question V198: Justifiable: claiming government benefits. See http://www.worldvaluessurvey.org/wvs.jsp.

9. Jean-Baptiste Michau, "Unemployment Insurance and Cultural Transmission: Theory and Application to European Unemployment," CEP Discussion Paper No. 936, Centre for Economic Performance, London School of Economics and Political Science, London, UK (2009).

10. Martin Halla, Mario Lackner, and Friedrich G. Schneider, *An Empirical Analysis of the Dynamics of the Welfare State: The Case of Benefit Morale*, IZA DP No. 4165 (Institute for the Study of Labor, 2010), 14, http://ftp.iza.org/dp4165.pdf.

11. Assar Lindbeck, "Hazardous Welfare-State Dynamics," *American Economic Review* 85, no. 2 (1995): 9–15; Assar Lindbeck, "Prospects for the Welfare State," seminar paper no. 755, Stockholm: Institute for International Economic Studies, Stockholm University, January 31, 2008.

12. Lindbeck, "Prospects for the Welfare State." It is worth noting that Nordic countries have relatively large shadow economies compared with countries such as the United States. Scandinavian shadow economies have reduced as a share of total GDP over time, coinciding with a shift towards greater economic freedom: see Friedrich Schneider and Colin C. Williams, *The Shadow Economy* (London: Institute of Economic Affairs, 2013), http://www.iea.org.uk/sites/default/files/publications/files/IEA%20Shadow%20 Economy%20web%20rev%207.6.13.pdf.

13. Arne Modig and Kristina Broberg, Är det OK att sjukskriva sig om man inte är sjuk? (Stockholm, TEMO, 2002), http://www.svensktnaringsliv.se/migration_catalog/ ar-det-ok-att-sjukskriva-sig-fast-man-inte-ar-sjuk_525675.html/binary/%C3%84r%20 det%20OK%20att%20sjukskriva%20sig%20fast%20man%20inte%20 %C3%A4r%20sjuk-.

14. Peter Skogman Thoursie, "Reporting Sick: Are Sporting Events Contagious?" *Journal of Applied Econometrics* 19 (2004): 809–23.

15. Malin Persson, *Korta sjukskrivningar under fotbolls VM 2002—en empirisk studie* (Nationalekonomiska Institutionen, Uppsala University, 2005). In both cases, the sickness rate among women is used as a control for other variations.

16. M. Ljunge, "Yngre generationers högre sjukskrivningstal—ett mått på hur snabbt välfärdsstaten förändrar normer," *Ekonomisk Debatt* 5 (2013): 56–61. Translated from Swedish.

17. Carl Hunnerup Dahl, *"Velfærdsstat og Arbejdsmoral,"* (Welfare and Work Ethic), YouTube video, 42:06, from the event "Welfare and Work Ethic," recorded in CEPOS' tent under Folkemødet on Bornholm, posted by CEPOSdk, June 21, 2013, https://www. youtube.com/watch?v=8YnVZzWYKmw&noredirect=1. Translated from Danish. See also Suzanne Daly, "Danes Rethink a Welfare State Ample to a Fault," *New York Times*, April 20, 2013, http://www.nytimes.com/2013/04/21/world/europe/danes-rethink-a-welfare-state-ample-to-a-fault.html.

18. Amalie Kestler, *"Corydon: Konkurrencestat er Ny Velfærdsstat"* (Corydon: Competition State's new welfare), *Politiken*, August 23, 2013. Own translation from Danish.

19. Økonomi og indenrigsministeriet (Economy and Ministry of Interior), Økonomisk redegørelse (Economic Survey), August 2013, http://www.fm.dk/publikationer/2013/ oekonomisk-redegoerelse-august-2013.

20. See more in Nima Sanandaji, "The Dutch Rethink the Welfare State," *New Geography*, November 2, 2013, http://www.newgeography.com/content/004028-the-dutch-rethink-welfare-state.

21. In the 2015 election the British conservatives, which during their previous term in government had limited welfare programs extensively, won reelection. To the surprise of the world, the conservatives increased their seats so that they were able to form a majority government, instead of the coalition government that they had previously formed together with the centrist Liberal Democrats.

22. Richard Milne, "Norway: Cruise Control," *Financial Times*, February 6, 2014, http://www.ft.com/cms/s/0/abe0f6f6-8f0c-11e3-9cb0-00144feab7de.html#axzz46pwtGZrg.

23. "Svensk arbetsmoral utklassar norrmännens," *Dagens Möjligheter*, November 14, 2012.

24. Vegard Skjervheim, *"En «trygdesnylters» bekjennelser"* ("The Confessions of a 'Welfare Freeloader'"), *Dagbladet*, 2012, http://www.dagbladet.no/2012/03/31/kultur/debatt/nav/trygdesnylter/20924592/.

25. Gordon B. Dahl, Andreas Ravndal Kostøl, and Magne Mogstad, "Family Welfare Cultures," *Quarterly Journal of Economics* 129 (2014): 1711–52.

26. Ibid.

27. Robert W. Fogel, "Catching Up with the Economy," *American Economic Review* 89, no. 1 (March 1999): 13, http://www.die-gdi.de/fileadmin/user_upload/pdfs/messner/Fogel_Catching_up_with_the_economy.pdf.

28. Reagan, Radio Address to the Nation on Welfare Reform.

CHAPTER 9: WHERE DOES THE AMERICAN DREAM COME TRUE?

1. Blake Fleetwood, "If You Want the American Dream, Go to Finland," *HuffPost Politics: The Blog*, December 14, 2013, http://www.huffingtonpost.com/blake-fleetwood/finland-2_b_4373187.html.

2. Raymond Freeman, "Nordic Reality vs. American Dream," *VC Reporter*, June 12, 2014, http://www.vcreporter.com/cms/story/detail/nordic_reality_vs_american_dream/12033/ .

3. Ann Jones, "Op-Ed: The American Way over the Nordic Model? Are We Crazy?" *Los Angeles Times*, January 11, 2015, http://www.latimes.com/nation/la-oc-0111-jones-ex-pat-american-20150111-story.html.

4. "Real American Dream More Possible in Norway," *Nordic Page*, September 24, 2013, http://www.tnp.no/norway/politics/3987-real-american-dream-more-possible-in-norway.

5. Nick Haekkerup and William Milberg, "The American Dream Comes to Life in Denmark," *Public Seminar*, October 22, 2013, http://www.publicseminar.org/2013/10/the-american-dream-comes-to-life-in-denmark/.

6. Tove Lifvendahl, "Världens Mest Attraktiva Invandrarland Är Inte Sverige" (The World's Most Attractive Immigration Country Is Sweden) *Svenska Dagbladet*, February 29, 2016, http://www.svd.se/varldens-mest-attraktiva-invandrarland-ar-inte-sverige, translated from Swedish.

7.   James Truslow Adams, *The Epic of America*, 2nd ed. (Greenwood Press, 1931), 404.

8.   Jeremy Rifkin, *The European Dream: How Europe's Vision of the Future Is Quietly Eclipsing the American Dream*, new ed. (New York: Tarcher, 2004), 38.

9.   See for example Anders Björklund et al., "Brother correlations in earnings in Denmark, Finland, Norway and Sweden compared to the United States," *Journal of Population Economics* 15, no. 4 (November 2002): 757–72; and Jo Blanden, Paul Gregg, and Stephen Machin, "Intergenerational Mobility in Europe and North America: A Report Supported by the Sutton Trust," Centre for Economic Performance, April 2005, http://cep.lse.ac.uk/about/news/IntergenerationalMobility.pdf.

10. Markus Jäntti et al., "American Exceptionalism in a New Light: A Comparison of Intergenerational Earnings Mobility in the Nordic Countries, the United Kingdom and the United States," IZA Discussion Paper no. 1938, January 2006, p. 2, http://ftp.iza.org/dp1938.pdf.

11. Tom Hertz, "A Group-Specific Measure of Intergenerational Persistence," *Economics Letters* 100, no 3 (2008): 415–17.

12. Deborah Roseveare and Martin Jorgensen, "Migration and Integration of Immigrants in Denmark," OECD Economics Department Working Papers, no. 386, 2004, http://dx.doi.org/10.1787/284832633602; Emma Carmel, Alfio Cerami, and Theodoros Papadopoulos, *Migration and Welfare in the New Europe: Social Protection and the Challenges of Integration* (Bristol, UK: Policy Press, 2011); and Laird, "Unemployment among Mexican Immigrant Men in the United States, 2003-2012," *Social Science Research* 49. (2014): 202–16.

13. Benny Carlsson, Karin Magnusson, and Sofia Rönnqvist, *Somalier på arbetsmarknaden— har Sverige något att lära?* (Swedish Government, 2012), http://www.regeringen.se/contentassets/55f58b2bc8fd4f66842e37f54c38fc51/somalier-pa-arbetsmarknaden---har-sverige-nagot-att-lara.

14. Silje Vatne Pettersen and Lars Østby, "Immigrants in Norway, Sweden and Denmark: Scandinavian Comparative Statistics on Integration," Statistics Norway, 2014, https://www.ssb.no/en/befolkning/artikler-og-publikasjoner/_attachment/204333?_ts=1497ab86428.

15. Kristian Rose Tronstad, "Integration and Experienced Discrimination of NonWestern Immigrants in the Norwegian Labor Market," paper presented at QMSS2 Seminar on "Measuring Integration and Discrimination," Paris, July 5–6, 2010.

16. Svein Blom and Kristen Henriksen, *Living Conditions among Immigrants in Norway 2005/2006*, (Statistics Norway, 2009), http://www.ssb.no/a/english/publikasjoner/pdf/rapp_200902_en/rapp_200902_en.pdf.

17. Swedish Government, *Egenförsörjning eller Bidragsförsörjning?—Invandrarna, Arbetsmarknaden och Välfärdsstaten* (Own Supplies or Grants Livelihood? Immigrants, Labor Market and Welfare State) (Stockholm, SOU, 2004:21), http://www.regeringen.se/contentassets/2900e981c8e84a8cae98d6f35c4641dd/egenforsorjning-eller-bidragsforsorjning-invandrarna-arbetsmarknaden-och-valfardsstaten.

18. SCB and Arbetslivsinstitutet, "Integration till svensk välfärd? Om invandrarnas välfärd på 90-talet" (Integration towards Swedish Living Standards? Living Conditions of Immigrants to Sweden in the 1990s), *Levnadsförhållanden* no. 96 (2002), http://www.scb.se/statistik/LE/LE0101/2000I02/LE96S%C3%850201.pdf.

19. United States Census Bureau, "Census 2000 Foreign Born Profiles," accessed April 25, 2016, https://www.census.gov/population/foreign/data/stp-159-2000.html.

20. Vahid Garousi, "Iranians in Canada: A Statistical Analysis" (PhD Thesis, Department of Systems and Computer Engineering, Carleton University, 2005), http://iranian.com/News/2005/June/IraniansCanada.pdf.

21. Statistics Canada. Calculations based on the 2006 survey.

22. Dan-Olof Rooth, "Refugee Immigrants in Sweden: Educational Investment and Labor Market Integration," *Lund Economic Studies* no. 84. (1999), http://lup.lub.lu.se/record/39980.

23. Assaf Razin and Jackline Wahba, "Free vs. Controlled Migration: Bilateral Country Study," NBER Working Paper no. 16831, February 2011, p. 2, http://www.nber.org/papers/w16831.pdf. See also Alon Cohen and Assaf Razin, "The Skill Composition of Immigrants and the Generosity of the Welfare State: Free vs. Policy-Controlled Migration," NBER Working Paper no. 14459, October 2008, http://www.nber.org/papers/w14459.pdf.

24. This has been shown for international sports stars, among others. States and countries with low taxes are more appealing to these athletes, which explains why their teams tend to be more successful. See, for example, Peter Egger and Doina Maria Radulescu, "The Influence of Labour Taxes on the Migration of Skilled Workers," *World Economy* 32, no. 9 (August 2009): 1365–79; Edda Claus and Iris Claus, "The Effects of Taxation on Migration: Some Evidence for the ASEAN and APEC Economies," *Asian Development Review* 28, no. 1 (2010): 22–50; and Kopkin, "Tax Avoidance: How Income Tax Rates Affect the Labor Migration Decisions of NBA Free Agents," *Journal of Sports Economics* 13, no. 6 (2012): 571–602.

25. World Value Survey 2010–2014.

26. Andreas Bergh, "Labour-Market Integration of Immigrants in OECD-Countries: What Explanations Fit the Data?" ECIPE Occasional Paper, no. 4/2013, available online at http://ecipe.org/publications/labour-market-integration-immigrants-oecd-countries-what-explanation-fit-data/.

27. Peter Nannestad, "Immigration as a Challenge to the Danish Welfare State?" *European Journal of Political Economy* 20 (2004): 755–67. http://www.biu.ac.il/soc/ec/seminar/data/immig.pdf.

28. OECD, *OECD Economic Surveys Denmark* (Paris: OECD, 2003). http://www.keepeek.com/Digital-Asset-Management/oecd/economics/oecd-economic-surveys-denmark-2003_eco_surveys-dnk-2003-en#page1.

29. Tronstad, "Integration and Experienced Discrimination of NonWestern Immigrants in the Norwegian Labor Market."

30. Bjørgulf Claussen, Lisbeth Smeby, and Dag Bruusgaard, "Disability Pension Rates among Immigrants in Norway," *Journal of Immigrant and Minority Health* 14, no. 2 (2012): 259–63.

31. My calculations were based on subtracting the share reported to be in good health from 100 percent (data for 2009).

32. See, for example, Michal Molcho et al. "Health and Well-Being among Child Immigrants in Europe," *Eurohealth* 16, no. 1 (2010): 20–23, http://www.lse.ac.uk/ LSEHealthAndSocialCare/pdf/eurohealth/VOL16No1/Molcho.pdf; and Björn Albin et al., "County Differences in Mortality among Foreign-Born Compared to Native Swedes 1970–1999," *Nursing Research and Practice* (2012).

33. Data on "indicators of integration of immigrants and their children" accessed February 20, 2016, from http://www.oecd.org/migration/integrationindicators, for the years 2009–2010, for fifteen- to sixty-four-year-olds.

34. See, for example, Pettersen and Østby, "Immigrants in Norway, Sweden and Denmark."

35. Gordon B. Dahl, Andreas Ravndal Kostol, and Magne Mostad, "Family Welfare Cultures," NBER Working Paper no. 19237, July 2013.

CHAPTER 10: SWEDEN'S SELF-INFLICTED IMMIGRATION CRISIS

1. Benjamin J. Tetelbaum, "Sweden's Self-Inflicted Nightmare," Opinion Pages, *New York Times*, November 13, 2015, http://www.nytimes.com/2015/11/14/opinion/swedens-self-inflicted-nightmare.html?mwrsm=Facebook.

2. Griff Witte and Anthony Faiola, "Even Europe's Humanitarian Superpower Is Turning Its Back on Refugees," *Washington Post*, December 30, 2015, https:// www.washingtonpost.com/world/europe/even-sweden-is-turning-its-back-on-refugees/2015/12/30/6d7e8454-a405-11e5-8318-bd8caed8c588_story.html.

3. Kristoffer Orstadius, *"Tio År Senare Har Varannan Mindre Än 13000 i månaden"* (Ten years later, every second less than 13,000 a month), *Dagens Nyheter*, March 4, 2015, http://www.dn.se/nyheter/sverige/tio-ar-senare-har-varannan-mindre-an-13-000-i-manaden-1/.

4. "Sweden: Something Souring in Utopia," *Time*, July 19, 1976, http://content.time.com/ time/subscriber/article/0,33009,914329-3,00.html.

5. The word "liberal" doesn't have quite the same meaning in Swedish politics as in American.

6. Tino Sanandaji, *Utanförskapets karta—en uppföljning av Folkpartiets rapportserie* (New report: "Level of social exclusion map—a follow-up of the Liberal Party's report series") (Stockholm: New Welfare Foundation, 2014), http://www.dnv.se/wp-content/ uploads/2014/05/Utanf%C3%B6rskapets-karta-en-uppf%C3%B6ljning-.pdf.

7. Ibid. Mauricio Rojas, a Chilean-Swedish intellectual, who had developed the first version of the report for the Liberal Party, explained in the foreword that the Liberal Party had stopped mapping the development of socially marginalized city parts because they knew, or at least could guess, that the development had not stopped.

8. *"Polisens Larm: 'Vi Går På Knäna Nu'"* ("Police Alarm: 'We Go on Our Knees Now'"), SVT Nyheter, January 25, 2016, translated from Swedish, http://www.svt.se/nyheter/lokalt/stockholm/polisens-larm-vi-gar-pa-knana-nu.

9. *"Extrem situation jämfört med grannländerna"* ("Extreme situation in comparison with neighboring countries"), SVT Nyheter Väst, November 6 2015, http://www.svt.se/nyheter/lokalt/vast/extrem-situation-jamfort-med-grannlanderna.

10. Kellan Howell, "'60 Minutes' Australia Crew Attacked by Masked Men While Reporting on Refugee Crisis," *Washington Times*, March 1, 2016, http://www.washingtontimes.com/news/2016/mar/1/60-minutes-australia-crew-attacked-masked-men-whil/.

11. "Länsstyrelser varnar för krisläge om flyktingvågen fortsätter" ("The county Administrative Board Warns of Crisis If the Refugee Wave Continues" *Dagens Nyheter*, October 10, 2015, http://www.dn.se/nyheter/sverige/lansstyrelser-varnar-for-krislage-om-flyktingvagen-fortsatter/.

12. Starta Bildspel, "Madrasserna slut i hela skåne" ("The Mattresses out in Skåne"), *Aftonbladet*, October 8, 2015, http://www.aftonbladet.se/nyheter/paflykt/article21550808.ab.

13. Toppnyheter, "Flyktingpojke misstänks vara 45 år gammal—åtalas för våldtäkt på 12-åring" ("Refugee boy suspected to be 45 years old—to be prosecuted for rape of 12-year-old"), Växjö Nyheter, February 18, 2016, http://vaxjonyheter.se/flyktingpojke-misstanks-vara-45-ar-gammal-atalas-for-valdtakt-pa-12-aring/.

14. "Stöd till ensamkommande ökar kraftigt," TV4 News, March 30, 2016. http://www.tv4.se/nyheterna/klipp/st%C3%B6d-till-ensamkommande-%C3%B6kar-kraftigt-3321592.

15. Olle Lönnaeus, *"Löfven: Svårt att regera utan DÖ"* ("Löfven: Hard to reign without DYING"), *Sydsvenskan*, April 29, 2015, http://www.sydsvenskan.se/skane/lofven-svart-att-regera-utan-do/.

16. Romson resigned in May 2016, following a scandal in which leading members of the Environmental Party were accused of having Islamist sympathies. During this scandal she referred to the 9/11 terrorist attacks as the "September 11th accidents," since they had caused anti-Muslim sentiments.

17. David Crouch, "Sweden Slams Shut Its Open-Door Policy towards Refugees," *Guardian*, November 24, 2015, http://www.theguardian.com/world/2015/nov/24/sweden-asylum-seekers-refugees-policy-reversal.

18. Gabriel Heller Sahlgren, *"Invandringen och Sveriges Resultatfall i Pisa"* ("Immigration and Sweden's Earnings Drop in Pisa"), Research Institute of Industrial Economics, Policy Paper no. 71 (July 2015).

19. Ibid.

20. OECD (2015).

21. "Tillsyn i Ross Tensta Gymnasium," Swedish School Inspection, 2016, translated from Swedish.

CHAPTER 11: WHERE ARE NORDIC SOCIETIES HEADING?

1. "Danish PM in US: Denmark is not socialist," the *Local*, November 1, 2015, http://www.thelocal.dk/20151101/danish-pm-in-us-denmark-is-not-socialist.

2. OECD, Benefits and Wages: Statistics. Over a five-year period following unemployment, 2001–2013. Re-trieved February 26, 2016.

3. To repeat a fact stated previously in this book: the average person in Sweden is paying a total tax rate of 52 percent. But when Swedes are asked, on average they estimate the tax burden to be around 34 percent. Nima Sanandaji, *"Underskattade Skatter—en Undersökning av vad Svenska Folket Tror om Skatternas Omfattning"* (Understated Taxes—an Examination of What the Swedish People Think about Taxes Extent), Confederation of Swedish Enterprise, August 2015, http://www.svensktnaringsliv.se/material/rapporter/underskattade-skatter-en-undersokning-av-vad-svenska-folket-tror_624361.html. Keep in mind that the tax level on the average individual tends to be higher than the tax level as a share of GDP. The simple reason is that all economic activity is not taxed as heavily as work is. For example, capital is typically taxed based on a lower rate, and with more deductions, than work.

4. Martin Pengelly, "Bernie Sanders Calls for 'Political Revolution' against Billionaire Class," *Guardian*, May 3, 2015, http://www.theguardian.com/us-news/2015/may/03/bernie-sanders-political-revolution-billionaire-democratic-2016-race.

5. OECD Stat Extract. Top statutory personal income tax rate and top marginal tax rates for employees. Re-trieved February 26, 2016.

6. 2016 Index of Economic Freedom, Heritage Foundation website, http://www.heritage.org/index/, retrieved February 26, 2016.

Index

Note: The letter ⊤ following a page number denotes a table. The letter g following a page number denotes a graph.

A

absolute poverty rates (Nordics and United States, compared), 66
Adams, James Truslow, 147
affirmative action, 119, 120, 121
Afghanistan, 177
Ahern, Kenneth, 119
Ahlfors, Lars Valerian, 61
Alestalo, Matti, 115–16
American Dream, 3, 146–48, 150, 152, 155, 159, 165–66 (see in general chapter 9)
American exceptionalism, 149
American Left, 2, 18, 21, 23–24, 29, 67, 136, 198n18
Americans
    GDP per capita of, 63t
    high school graduation rate (age 25+) among, 64t
    number reporting Nordic/Scandinavian origins, 62
    unemployment rate among, 65t
Aristotle, 50
Arnold, Daniel, 201n22
Associated Press, 31

Atkinson, Anthony Barnes, 39
Atlantic, 47
Australia, 25t, 29, 33, 34t, 37
Austria, 37, 40t
Axelsson, Sten, 91

B

Back to Work (B. Clinton), 19
Barton, Arnold, 59
Beddy, James, 84–85
Belgium, 37n, 40t, 46t
benefit morale, 131, 133, 201n22
Benefit Street (documentary series), 139
Bennhold, Katrin, 107
Bergh, Andreas, 56–57, 159
Bertrand, Marianne, 119
Better Life Index, 24, 25t, 29, 198n19
Better Policies for Better Lives project, 163
Bjørnskov, Christian, 56–57
Blue-Blue Cabinet, 6
Borlaug, Norman, 60–61
Boston Globe, 23
Buchanan, James, 76
bumblebee analogy, 83, 104

C

California, 27

Canada, 25t, 34t, 37n, 38, 155

capitalism, 5, 18, 24, 86, 87, 88, 110, 148, 190–92

Center Left, the, 168, 196n3

Center Right, the, 196n3
    center-right coalition/government, 5, 7, 93, 96, 107, 168, 172

CEPOS (Center for Politiske Studier), 73

child care / day care, 4, 17, 23, 108, 111, 114, 116, 162, 192

child mortality, 35–38

China, 2

choices, role in social outcomes, 33

Chydenius, Anders, 87

Civil War, 59, 61

climate, 29, 49, 51, 53, 84, 85, 158

Clinton, Bill, 19, 130

Clinton, Hillary, 9, 18–19, 23, 31, 126

CNN, 20, 196n1

coffee, 47–49

Cold War, 61

collective bargaining, 159. *See also* labor union(s)

Columbus, Christopher, 53

competition, 71, 116, 138, 187, 189

Confederation of Swedish Enterprise, 73, 118

Conservative Party (in Norway), 5, 6

Corydon, Bjarne, 136, 137

country, -ies. *See individual countries by name; see also* Nordic country
    characteristics of high-trust, 54
    growth by country during
        the early social democrat era (1936–1970), 89t
        the free-market era (1870–1936), 88t
        the new market-reform era (1991–2014), 95t
        the Third Way Socialist era (1970–1991), 94t
    top ten. *See* top ten countries

crime, 24, 173, 174, 175, 179, 181, 182

Cross-Cultural Business Behavior (Gesteland), 47

Cuba, 2

culture, 9, 10, 11, 12, 13, 29, 33, 34, 39, 41, 48–49, 50, 54, 56, 57, 58, 62, 66, 68, 74, 85, 86, 99, 120, 131, 132, 139, 140, 142, 149, 153, 158, 172, 175, 181–82, 193, 194
    the main ingredient of Nordic success, 68
    role of, in life expectancy (in Iceland, Denmark), 11, 34
    role of, in social outcomes, 33
    coldness of Scandinavian, 158

Czech Republic, 37n, 39–40

D

Dahl, Casper Hunnerup, 135

Dahl, Gordon B., 141–42

Dagens Nyheter (Swedish daily newspaper), 170–71

Dagens Samhälle (Swedish magazine), 9

Danes, 17, 31–32, 34–35, 47, 62, 69, 135, 136, 160. *See* Denmark

Danish Americans, 62, 65, 66
    GDP per capita among, 63t
    high school graduation rate (age 25+) among, 64t
    number of, 202n5
    poverty rate in the United States among, 66t
    unemployment rate among, 65t

Danish People's Party, 6

day care. *See* child care

DeLamater, Cornelius, 61

Delhey, Jan, 53–54

democratic socialism, 4, 5, 6, 7, 10, 18, 19, 57, 90, 93, 95, 96, 102, 104, 112, 118, 166, 185, 189, 192. *See also* social democracy; socialism

Democrats, 19, 130

de Neubourg, Chris, 65–66

Denmark, 2, 3, 5, 6, 11, 13, 17–19, 24, 25t, 31–35, 36, 37t, 39, 40, 45, 46t, 52, 62, 66, 70, 71, 72, 74, 83, 84–86, 93, 94, 105, 115, 116, 130, 136–38, 146, 147, 150, 152, 160, 173, 184, 185–86t, 187, 188, 189, 190, 191t, 193, 199nn3–5, 201n14. *See also* Danes.

  absolute poverty rate in, 66

  coffee consumption per person in the, 48t

  difference in unemployment between high-educated native born and foreign born in, 157t

  employment levels comparing foreign native born to foreign born in, 151t

  GDP per capita in, 63t

  high school graduation rate (age 25+) in, 64t

  percent of women employees employed in the public sector, 115

  PISA scores of children of immigrants in, 164t

  ranking on the Better Life Index, 25t

  ranking on list of top ten countries with lowest income inequality, 40t

  rate of growth during

    early social democrat era (1936–1970), 89t

    free market era (1870–1936), 88t

    Third Way Socialist era (1970–1991), 94t

  share of immigrants who self-identify as not in good health, 163

  share of women managers in, 112t

  top tax rate in, 189t

  total tax rate in 1960, 199n4

  unemployment rate in, 65t

  unemployment levels between low-educated native born and foreign born in, 153t

Detroit, 173

disability insurance, 142

disability pension, 162

Dittmar, Amy, 119

divorce, 109

Doerrenberg, Philipp, 74

Dregni, Eric, 59, 60

Du Rietz, Anita Lignell, 111

E

early retirement, 102, 103, 136, 162, 206n26

economies, perfect starting point for successful, 54

Economist, 90

Edling, Jan, 102–3

egalitarianism, 45, 107, 109

elderly care, 2, 118, 147, 162, 189

employee funds, 91, 92–93

employer, share of workers in Europe totally committed to their, 46t

employer's fee, 75

Environmental Party, 169, 178, 215n16

Epic of America, The (Adams), 147

equality, 11, 21, 22, 38–40, 147. *See also* gender equality

entrepreneurship, 71, 72, 86, 90, 91, 94, 104, 115, 117, 151

Erickson, George, 60

Ericsson (Swedish corporation), 88

Ericsson, John, 61

Ericsson, Peter, 73

Europe, share of workers "totally committed to their employer," 46t

European Central Bank, 72

European Dream, The (Rifkin), 147–48

European Union, 6, 108, 203n12, 203n2 (chap. 5)

Eurostat, 108, 112, 202n8

F

Faiola, Anthony, 168
fairness, 22, 45
Febiger, Hans Christian, 61
Feldt, Kjell Olof, 92–93
feminism, 113
Ferdman, Roberto, 47
Field of Dreams (movie), 26
Financial Times, 140
Finland, 5, 6, 13, 19, 24, 25t, 30, 32, 36,
    37t, 40t, 45, 48–49, 51, 52, 62, 66,
    72, 101, 105, 116, 138, 146, 164, 173,
    188, 199nn3–5
  coffee consumption per person in the, 48t
  GDP per capita, 63t
  high school graduation rate (age 25+)
    among, 64t
  PISA scores of children of immigrants in,
    164t
  total tax rate in 1960, 199n4
  unemployment rate in, 65t
Finnish Americans, 62, 66
  GDP per capita among, 63t
  high school graduation rate (age 25+)
    among, 64t
  number of, 202n5
  poverty rate in the United States among,
    66t
  unemployment rate among, 65t
Finns Party, 6
First World War, 91
Fischbacher, Fehr and Urs, 127
Fleetwood, Blake, 146
Flood, Lennart, 73
Fogel, Robert, 144
Fox News, 7
France, 11, 26, 34t, 37t, 38, 46t, 112, 114
fraud (benefit), 133
Freeman, Raymond, 146

free-market era, growth of various countries
    during the, 88t
free-market policies, 84, 86, 101
Fregert, Klas, 101
Friedman, Milton, 67

G

gangs, 8, 173, 174, 176
GDP (gross domestic product), 30, 31, 54,
    63, 75, 199n5, 203n9, 210n12, 216n3
gender equality, 106–9, 111, 112, 118
gender gap, 115
Gender and Jobs (International Labour
    Office), 115
Germany, 46t, 114, 138
Global Gender Gap report, 106
Great Depression, 55, 97–99, 125, 206n21
Greece, 26, 37n
Green Revolution, 61
Greens, 196n8
Gripenstedt, Johan August, 87
gross domestic product (GDP), 30, 54
growth by country during
    the early social democrat era (1936–
      1970), 89t
    the free-market era (1870–1936), 88t
    the new market-reform era (1991–2014),
      95t
    the Third Way Socialist era (1970–1991),
      94t
Grytten, Ola Honningdal, 99
Guardian (UK), 108, 178
Gunnlaugsson, Sigmundur Davíð (prime
    minister, Iceland), 5

H

Haekkerup, Nick, 147
Halla, Martin, 132
Hammarstedt, Mats, 179
Hansson, Åsa, 72

hard left, 94
hard work, 12, 49, 50, 52, 59, 60, 71, 117, 131, 140, 149
health, share of immigrants who identify themselves as not in good, 163t
Hayek, Friedrich, 22
H&M (Swedish company), 88, 91, 144
Heinemann, Friedrich, 128, 130–31
Henrekson, Magnus, 90, 114
Heritage Foundation, 5, 190
hidden unemployment, 97, 102–4
higher education, 3, 156, 162, 170, 192, 202n8
Hilton, Conrad (founder of Hilton Hotels), 61
Hilton, James, 198n18
Hinnfors, Jonas, 9
Homestead Act of 1862, 59
honesty, 52, 59
Honkapohja, Seppo, 101
Hort, Sven E. O., 115–16
Huffington Post, 146
Hungary, 46t

I
Iceland, 5, 6, 11, 13, 24, 25t, 29–30, 32–33, 34, 35, 36, 37, 40, 45, 112, 173, 186, 188, 190, 192–93, 199nn3–5, 203n2
ideologues, 4, 5, 10, 12, 13, 18, 21, 26, 27, 40, 55, 185
IKEA, 88, 91
immigrants
    who identify themselves as not in good health, share of (by country), 163t
    PISA scores of the children of, 164t
Immigrants in American History (Barton), 59
immigration. *See in general chapter 10* (pp. 167–82); *also* 5, 6, 7–8, 12, 20, 86, 161, 183, 184
income equality, 11, 38–40, 54, 193

incomes, 38, 39, 40, 63, 72, 118, 137, 148, 149, 152, 155, 171, 188, 200n14
Index of Economic Freedom, 5, 190
individual responsibility, 5, 12, 13, 27, 29, 33, 41, 50, 58, 131, 138, 140, 145, 149, 175, 182
inequality, 12, 20, 38–40, 165, 179, 184
Inquiry into the Nature and Causes of the Wealth of Nations, An (Smith), 87
International Labor Organization, 111
Iran, 3, 155, 176
Iranians, 154, 155, 157
Iraqis, 156, 157
Ireland, 37n, 46t, 84–86
Islamic terrorism, 173
Israel, 34t
Italy, 11, 26, 34t, 37t, 46t

J
Jackson, Gabrielle, 108
Jäntti, Markus, 148
Japan, 33, 34t, 37
Jefferson, Thomas, 51, 201n15
jobs (Sweden)
    growth in public, private sectors, 96, 97g
    main reason for private service sector's failure to create new, 100
Johnson, Anders, 110
Johnson, Clarence Leonard, 61
Jones, Ann, 146–47
journalists, 21, 22, 26, 67, 69, 170, 171, 174, 179

K
Kamp, David, 47
Klein, Ezra, 18–19
Kleven, Henrik Jacobsen, 27–28, 70, 73–74
Korea, 37
Koskela, Erkki, 101

Kostøl, Andreas Ravndal, 141–42
Krugman, Paul, 22, 23
Kuhnle, Stein, 115–16
Kurdi, Alan, 168

L

labor market regulations, 94, 100, 170, 192
labor union(s), 18, 91, 117, 159, 161, 166
Lackner, Mario, 132
Laffer, Arthur, 71
Larsson, Stieg, 47
Lawrence, John Hundale, 61
Left, the, 2–4, 6, 18, 21, 29, 67, 69–70, 90,
   139, 196n8. *See also* American Left
leftist ideologues, 4, 5, 10, 12, 13, 18, 21,
   26, 40
Liberal Democrats (Brit.), 211n21
Liberal Party (in Sweden), 171, 172, 214n7
liberals (American), 6, 83
libertarians, 13, 136
Libertarians (US), 130
life expectancy, 10–11, 32–36
Lilyhammer (TV series), 140
Lindbeck, Assar, 50, 133
Liptak, Kevin, 20–21
living standard, 1, 18, 21, 24, 29, 50, 62–63,
   67, 84, 177, 187, 199n3
Ljunge, Martin, 134–35
Ljungqvist, Lars, 103
Löfven, Stefan, 147, 178
Logue, John, 22
Lord of the Rings, 34
Los Angeles Times, 146–47
lottery, 19
Lowry, Rich, 23–24, 198n18
Lundgren, Roger, 7
Luxembourg, 46t

M

Maine (and women's property rights), 110
Malmö (Sweden), 8, 174
Malte-Brun, Conrad, 52–53
marginalized city parts, 171, 172, 214n7
Massachusetts (and women's property
   rights), 110
McKinsey & Company, 100, 102
Metso Paper, 99
Michau, Jean-Baptiste, 132
Middle East, 162. *See also* Iran; Iranians;
   Iraqis; Saudi Arabia
Milgrom, Eva Meyersson, 117
Miliband, Ed, 146
minimum wage, 7, 129, 159
Mogstad, Magne, 141–42
Monde, Le (Paris), 23
monopolies, 2, 4, 6, 111, 116–18
Morocco, 173
Mothers' Index Rankings, 24

N

Nannestad, Peter, 159–60
National Gain, The (Chydenius), 87
National Public Radio, 83
National Review, 23
Netherlands, 34t, 37t, 38, 46t, 138
New Sweden, 59
Newton, Kenneth, 53–54
New Welfare Foundation, 172
New York Times, 47, 107, 167
New Zealand, 25t, 34t
9/11 terrorist attacks, 215n16
Nohab Flight, 98–99
Nordic Americans, 29, 57, 60, 62–67, 71 ,
   74, 193, 203n9
Nordic country
   with the largest tax burden in the world,
   5

with the largest share of women managers, 112t

with the smallest welfare state, 32–33

Nordic Innovation Centre, 115

Nordic Labour Journal, 120

Nordic Model, The (Alestalo, Hort, and Kuhnle), 115–16

Nordic society, long-standing features of (that predate the welfare state), 27

Nordic success, 153

    four primary underpinnings of, 52

    main ingredient of, 68

    predates large welfare states. *See chapter 2* (pp. 26–41)

Nordic welfare states, 3–4, 13, 22, 24, 31, 33, 39, 102, 107, 108, 145, 157, 162, 198n18. *See also individual countries by name*

norms, 51, 52, 53, 55, 58, 106, 110, 111, 112, 127, 128, 131–32, 133, 135–36, 139, 140, 153, 187, 194

North Africa, 162, 173

North Korea, 2

Norway, 2, 3, 5, 13, 19, 24, 30, 32, 33, 34t, 36, 37t, 39, 45, 46t, 61, 62, 64–65, 93, 105, 109, 116, 117, 118, 120, 139–41, 146, 147, 152, 154, 161, 162, 173, 186t, 187, 188, 191t, 199nn3–5, 202n7, 203n12, 203n2 (chap. 5)

    coffee consumption per person in the, 48t

    difference in unemployment between high-educated native born and foreign born in, 157t

    employment levels comparing foreign native born to foreign born in, 151t

    GDP per capita in, 63t

    high school graduation rates among those 25 or older in, 64t

    PISA scores of children of immigrants in, 164t

    ranking on the Better Life Index, 25t

    ranking on list of top ten countries with lowest income inequality, 40t

    rate of growth during

        early social democrat era (1936–1970), 89t

        free market era (1870–1936), 88t

        Third Way Socialist era (1970–1991), 94t

    share of immigrants who self-identify as not in good health, 163

    top tax rate in, 189t

    total tax rate in 1960, 199n4

    unemployment levels between low-educated native born and foreign born in, 153t

    unemployment rate in, 65t

Norwegian Americans, 62, 66

    GDP per capita among, 63t

    high school graduation rate (age 25+) among, 64t

    number of, 202n5

    poverty rate in the United States among, 66t

    unemployment rate among, 65t

Norwegians, described, 53

Notten, Geranda, 65–66

O

Obama, Barack, 20–21

OECD, 24, 160, 199n3, 203n10. *See also* Better Life Index

Ohlin, Bertil, 76

oil, 5, 30, 62, 93, 104, 139, 141, 161, 199n3

Ojaniemi, Taija, 48–49

open borders, 6, 8, 169, 177, 178

Organization for Economic Cooperation and Development. *See* OECD

O'Rourke, Kevin, 85–86

P

parental leave, 18, 19, 31, 68, 107, 108, 111. *See also* paternal leave

paternity leave, 108, 114

payroll tax, 72, 203n5

Pehkonen, Jaakko, 101

Persson, Göran, 83

Petersen, Trond, 117

PISA (Program for International Student Assessment) global survey, 164, 180

PISA scores of the children of immigrants (by country), 180t

Poehler, Gregory (brother of *Saturday Night Live* star Amy Poehler), 158

Poland, 46t,

Popenoe, David, 22

Portugal, 37n, 46t

poverty, 3, 11–12, 22, 36, 53, 54, 60, 64, 65–68, 83, 129, 141–44, 165, 172, 179, 184, 193, 203n13

adopting welfare states does not remove, 11

rate within the United States, 66t

private sector, 95–97, 113, 115, 117, 200n1, 203n4

Progress Party (Norway), 6

property rights, 50–51, 86, 110

Protestant work ethic, 12, 50

Public Broadcasting Service (PBS), 31

public sector(s), 1, 4, 5, 11, 31, 32, 37, 39, 56, 58, 76, 95–97, 111, 114, 115–18, 128, 136, 189, 190, 191, 200n1, 203n4

public spending, 27, 138, 190

punctuality, 47, 52

Puviani, Amilcare, 76

Q

quotas, 118–20

R

Rasmussen, Lars Løkke (prime minister, Denmark), 5, 184, 185

Reagan, Ronald, 128–29, 130, 135, 139, 143, 144

reforms, 6, 84, 85, 87, 90, 96, 97, 101, 118, 133, 134, 137, 142, 170, 189, 193–94

refugees, 154, 168, 170–71, 175, 178

Reinfeldt, Fredrik, 20, 168–69

Renstig, Monica, 114

Republicans, 130

Rifkin, Jeremy, 147–48

Roine, Jesper, 38

Rojas, Mauricio, 214n7

Romson, Åsa, 178, 215n16

Roosevelt, Franklin D., 55, 125–26, 128, 130, 135, 139, 143, 144–45

Rubio, Marco, 7

Runeberg, Johan Ludvig, 51

Russia, 46t, 51, 207n7

S

SAAB, 99

Sachs, Jeffrey, 22

Saddam Hussein, 156

Sahlgren, Gabriel Heller, 180

Samuelson, Alexander, 61

Sanandaji, Tino, 12–13, 39, 169, 172, 180, 204n16

Sanders, Bernie, 1, 2–3, 7, 9, 12, 13, 17–18, 19, 26–27, 31, 55, 57, 126, 184, 187, 196n1, 197n10

Sargent, Thomas, 103

Saudi Arabia, 141

Save the Children, 24

Scandinavian Americans, 66, 68

GDP per capita among, 63t

high school graduation rate (age 25+) among, 64t

number of, 202n5
poverty rate in the United States among, 66t
unemployment rate among, 65t
Scandinavian business, role of Viking heritage (self-sufficiency, etc.) in, 45
Scandinavian Unexceptionalism (N. Sanandaji), 12, 13, 197n12
Schneider, Friedrich G., 132
Schyman, Gudrun, 113
Scientific American, 22
Seaborg, Glenn Theodore, 61
Second World War, 61
Securitas, 99
self-esteem, 144
self-reliance / self-sufficiency, 45, 125, 194
serfdom, 22, 39, 50
shadow economies, 210n12
Shangri-La (as an analogue), 23–24, 198n18
share of workers in Europe "totally committed to their employer," 46t
sick leave, 1, 7, 18, 32, 102, 103, 108, 134–35, 196n, 202n22, 207n26
Singapore, 33, 34t, 37
Sipilä, Juha Petri (prime minister, Finland), 5
60 Minutes, 174
Skjervheim, Vegard, 141
Skylitzes, John, 109
Slovak Republic, 39–41
Slovenia, 39–40
Smith, Adam, 87
Snartland, Vemund, 117
social capital, 53, 85, 86, 154
social cohesion, 24, 27, 54, 74, 86, 131, 140, 149, 175, 182
social democracy, 1–4, 18, 22, 24, 26, 27, 29, 30, 33, 35, 36, 41, 52, 55, 57, 62, 68, 70, 71, 79, 93, 102, 108, 120, 147, 149, 175, 182, 184, 187, 192 *See also* democratic socialism; socialism

American obsession with Nordic. *See chapter 1* (pp. 17–25)
core ideas of, 1
and socialism, compared, 2
Social Democrats/social democrats, 10g, 83, 89, 108, 185
in Denmark, 5, 136, 137, 184
in southern Europe, 27
in Sweden, 7, 8–9, 76, 89, 90, 92, 95, 178, 197n10
social engineering, 107–8
socialism, 2, 9, 24, 84, 86, 89, 91, 93, 94, 104, 120, 185, 191–93. *See also* democratic socialism; social democracy; Third Way
Socialists, 7, 9, 10g, 27
social mobility, 146, 148–49, 182
social outcomes, role of choices and culture in,
Søgaard, Jakob Egholt, 39
Solberg, Erna, 5
Somalia, 152, 154
Soviet Union, 2, 101
Spain, 4, 11, 34t
Spector, Susanne, 103
"spiritual resources," 144
sports events, increases in sickness absence during, 134
Springsteen, Bruce, 21
Statistics Canada, 155
Stenkula, Mikael, 114
Stockton, Robert, 61
Stoltenberg, Jens, 147
Sundback, Gideon, 61
Syria, 175, 176
Sweden, 2, 3, 6–9, 11–13, 19, 20, 21, 24, 31, 32, 33, 34t, 35, 36–39, 46t, 47, 52–53, 54, 59, 60, 62, 66, 71–75, 76, 83, 86–94, 96–105, 107–8, 109–18, 130, 131, 133–34, 136, 138, 143, 146, 147, 150, 152, 154–56, 158, 167–84,

186t, 187–90, 191t, 193, 199nn3–5, 204n16, 205n13, 206n26, 216n3

absolute poverty rate in, 66

breakdown of taxes paid by a wage earner in, 203n5

coffee consumption per person in the, 48t

difference in unemployment between high-educated native born and foreign born in, 157t

employment in

before and after the Great Depression, 98t

before and after the 1990s crisis, 100g

employment levels comparing foreign native born to foreign born in, 151t

GDP per capita in, 63t

high school graduation rate (age 25+) in, 64t

jobs growth (public-sector and private-sector) in, 96, 97g

immigration crisis in. See chapter 10 (pp. 167–82)

PISA scores of children of immigrants in, 164t

ranking on the Better Life Index, 25t

ranking on list of top ten countries with lowest income inequality, 40t

rate of growth during

early social democrat era (1936–1970), 89t

free market era (1870–1936), 88t

Third Way Socialist era (1970–1991), 94t

share of immigrants who self-identify as not in good health, 163

share of women managers in, 112t

top tax rate in, 189t

total tax rate in 1960, 199n4, 216n3

unemployment rate, 65t

unemployment levels between low-educated native born and foreign born in, 153t

Sweden Democrats, 7, 169, 178

Swedes, described, 52

Swedish Americans, 62, 66

GDP per capita among, 63t

high school graduation rate (age 25+) among, 64t

number of, 202n5

poverty rate in the United States among, 66t

unemployment rate among, 65t

Swedish Feminist Initiative, 113

Swedish Fiscal Policy Council, 179

Swedish School Inspectorate, 180–81

Swedish Trade Union Confederation LO, 102–3

Switzerland, 25t, 29, 33, 34t, 37t, 46t

T

tax. See in general chapter 5, "How Can the Nordics Tax So Much?" (pp. 69–79).

breakdown of taxes paid by a Swedish earner, 72–73, 203n5

employer's fee, 75

evolution of taxes in the Nordics over time. See graphs on pp. 77–78

top tax rate by country, 189

value-added tax (VAT), 75–76

on work and consumption, true level versus perceived (Swedes), 76, 79

tax reductions, 6, 11, 73, 96, 97, 188, 193

Teitelbaum, Benjamin, 167–68

Tennessee (and women's property rights), 110

Tetra Pak (Swedish company), 88, 91

Third Way, 24, 91–94, 192. See democratic socialism; social democracy

Time magazine, 21, 171

Tobin's Q, 119

top ten countries
    per Better Life Index, 25t
    with longest life span, 34t
    with lowest child mortality rates, 37t
    with lowest income inequality, 40t
Tocqueville, Alexis de, 149
Tronstad, Kristian Rose, 154, 161
Trump, Donald, 6
trust levels, 27, 28, 53–54, 55–57, 74, 85, 182
Turkey, 48, 155

U

UCLA, 112
Understanding Cross-Cultural Management (Browaeys and Price), 45
unemployment, 7, 18, 21, 26, 64–65, 67, 83, 97, 99, 101–4, 131, 132, 152–55, 157, 159, 161–62, 185, 206n26
    hidden, 97, 102–4
    how much more a single-earner family would make by working than by collecting, 186t
    unemployment rate by country or ethnic group, 65t
unemployment insurance, 160
United Kingdom, 34t, 37t, 46t, 114, 116, 138–39
United States, 4, 5, 6, 7, 12, 17, 18, 19, 20, 21, 28, 30–33, 36, 37n, 38, 40, 51, 52, 54–60, 63, 66, 69–70, 71, 74, 75, 86, 102, 110, 112, 114, 117, 139, 146–53, 155, 157, 158, 164, 165–66, 171, 185–88, 190–91, 196n1, 196n3, 199nn3–5, 200n14, 202n7, 203n9, 210n12
    coffee consumption per person in the, 48t
    difference in unemployment between high-educated native born and foreign born in, 157t
    employment levels comparing foreign native born to foreign born in, 151t
    GDP per capita in the, 63t
    PISA scores of children of immigrants in, 164t
    poverty rate within the, 66t
    ranking on the Better Life Index, 25t
    share of immigrants who self-identify as not in good health, 163
    share of women managers in, 112t
    total tax rate in 1960, 199n4
    unemployment levels between low-educated native born and foreign born in, 153t
universal health care, 10, 18, 23, 28, 31, 34, 38, 162
upward mobility, 12, 60, 148, 150, 164–66, 184
U.S. Census, 62, 155
USS *Monitor*; USS *Princeton*, 61

V

value-added tax (VAT), 75–76
Van Zandt, Steven, 140
VC Reporter, 146
Venezuela, 2
Vietnam War, 90
Vikings, 109, 207n7
Vikings (HBO series), 108–9
Vikings in the Attic (Dregni), 59
Volvo, 88
Volvo Aero (formerly Nohab Flight), 98–99
voter support for Social Democrats and Socialists in Swedish elections, 7, 10g
voucher systems, 118, 189
Vox, 18

W–X

wages, 7, 74, 117, 118, 119, 120, 156, 159, 161, 178, 184

Waldenström, Daniel, 38
Wallace, Björn, 204n16
Wall Street Journal, 5, 190
War on Poverty, 129
Washington, George, 61
Washington Post, 168
Washington Times, 174
Weber, Max, 50
Welcome to Sweden (comedy show), 158
welfare. *See in general chapter 8, "Generous Welfare Traps Families in Welfare Poverty"* (pp. 125–45). *See also* welfare dependencyl welfare states
    the most insidious effect of, 129
welfare dependency, 3, 8, 128, 129, 130, 131, 138, 139, 144, 154, 165, 171, 172, 175, 184, 192, 194
welfare states. *See in general chapter 8* (pp. 125–45)
    how benefits can reduce incentives to work and learn new skills, 159–60
    levels of trust in, 57
    Nordic success predates large. *See chapter 2* (26–41)
    role of, in social poverty, 144
    southern European, 26–27
    tendency to have rigid labor market laws, 151
    the truth about equality and, 38–41
    the truth about long life spans and, 31–35
    the truth about low child mortality and, 35–37
West Germany, 114
Witte, Griff, 168
women. *See chapter 7, "Why Are So Few Nordic Women at the Top?"* (pp. 106–21)
    managers, share of (by country), 112t
Women's Business Research Institute, 114
workers in Europe "totally committed to their employer," share of, 46t

work ethic(s), 5, 12, 13, 27, 28, 46, 49, 50, 54, 55, 59, 127, 128, 132, 133, 134, 135, 140, 145
World Economic Forum, 107
World Value Survey, 130–31, 158, 201n22

Y

young people (*also* the younger generation; young men, young women; youth), 71, 98, 134–35, 140, 144, 159, 172–73, 174, 204n16

Z

Zahidi, Saadia, 106–7

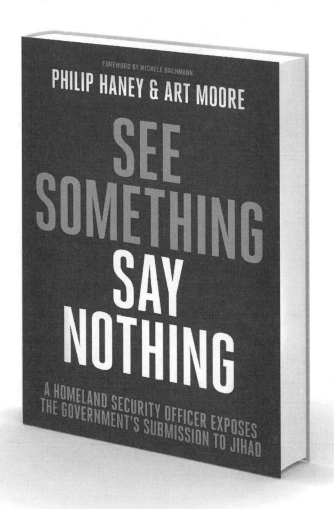

In SEE SOMETHING, SAY NOTHING, Haney and coauthor and veteran reporter Art Moore expose just how deeply the official submission, denial, and deception run. Haney's insider eyewitness account, supported by internal memos and documents, exposes a federal government capitulating to an enemy within and punishing those who reject its flawed narrative. As a result, the national campaign to raise public awareness of terrorism and terror-related crime known as "If You See Something, Say Something" has, in effect, morphed into "If You See Something, Say Nothing."

WND BOOKS • WASHINGTON DC • WNDBOOKS.COM

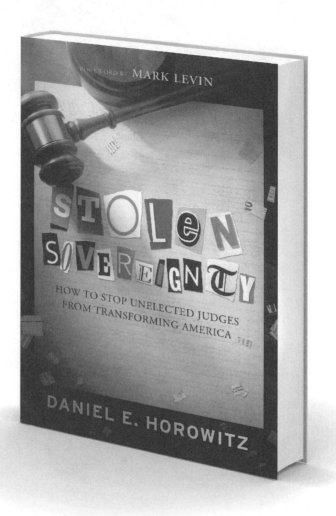

The Left has succeeded in so expanding the power of the courts and coopting them to serve as conduits for their radical ideas, that their rulings all but neuter the nation's legislatures and the will of the people. Even Americans' most sacred inalienable right, that of religious conscience, is under imminent threat of extinction. In STOLEN SOVEREIGNTY, you'll discover how our economy, society, culture, political system, safety, and security—and most prominently, our destiny—have been profoundly compromised.

WND Books • WASHINGTON DC • WNDBOOKS.COM

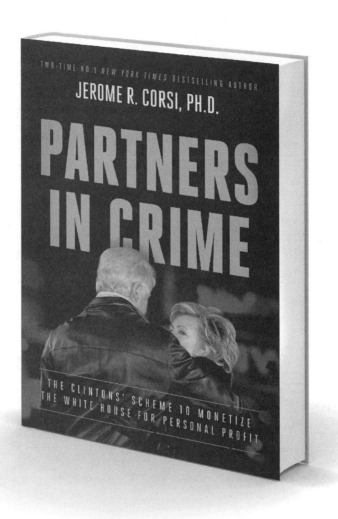

In PARTNERS IN CRIME, *New York Times* bestselling author Jerome Corsi presents the detailed research and expert testimony that proves beyond a shadow of a doubt that the Clinton Foundation is "a vast, criminal conspiracy." A slush fund for grifters, the Clintons have used the foundation as their own personal bank account and political scorecard. It is not enough for Hillary Clinton to withdraw from the 2016 presidential race in disgrace. Law enforcement authorities must close down the Clinton Foundation and end the crime spree once and for all.

WND BOOKS   •   WASHINGTON DC   •   WNDBOOKS.COM

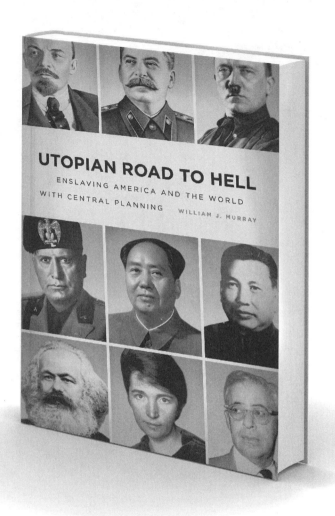

UTOPIAN ROAD TO HELL

ENSLAVING AMERICA AND THE WORLD
WITH CENTRAL PLANNING

WILLIAM J. MURRAY

Utopian dreamers are both deceived and deceitful. Their "fight for the people" rhetoric may sound good at first, but history proves egalitarian governments destroy freedom, destroy creativity, and destroy human lives. In UTOPIAN ROAD TO HELL, William J. Murray, son of former atheist apologist Madelyn Murray O'Hair, masterfully exposes the wide swath of destruction such deluded leaders have created throughout history and warns of the dangers posed by today's power-obsessed utopians.

WND Books • WASHINGTON DC • WNDBOOKS.COM